THE UNOFFICIAL
BIG GREEN EGG
COOKBOOK

INCLUDES TASTY RECIPES OF MEAT, FISH, POULTRY, GAME FOR MAKING BBQ WITH YOUR CERAMIC GRILL

BY ADAM JONES

TABLE OF CONTENTS

INTRODUCTION

Where there is a smoke, there is a flavor. Smoking meat or making BBQ is not only a means of cooking but for some individuals and classy enthusiasts, this is a form of Art! Or dare I say a form of lifestyle! Enthusiasts all around the world have been experimenting and dissecting the secrets of perfectly smoked meat for decades now, and in our golden age, perhaps they have cracked it up completely!In our age, the technique of Barbequing or Smoking meat has been perfected to such a level, that a BBQ Grill is pretty much an essential amenity found in all backyard or sea-beach parties!

This is the drinking fountain for the more hip and adventurous people, who prefer to have a nice chat with their friends and families while smoking up a few batches of Burger Patty for them to enjoy. But here's the thing, while this art might seem as a very easy form of cooking which only requires you to flip meats over and over! Mastering it might be a little bit difficult if you don't know have the proper information with you. This guide is an essential book

for beginners who want to smoke meat without needing expert help from others. This book offers detailed guidance obtained by years of smoking meat, includes clear instructions and step-by-step directions for every recipe. This is the only guide you will ever need to professionally smoke a variety of food. The book includes photographs of every finished meal to make your job easier. Whether you are a beginner meat smoker or looking to go beyond the basics, the book gives you the tools and tips you need to start that perfectly smoked meat. Smoking is something has withstood the test of time, it will continue to stand the test of time for years to come. Not only is it a method to preserve your catch or kill, but it's also one of if not the best-tasting food there is.

CHAPTER-1 BEEF

COFFEE TOUCH SMOKED BEEF RIBS WITH LIGHT BOURBON SAUCE

(COOKING TIME 5 HOURS 30 MINUTES)

INGREDIENTS FOR 10 SERVINGS

- Beef ribs (6-lb., 2.7-kg.)

THE RUB

- Brown sugar - ¾ cup
- Salt - 1 ½ teaspoon
- Dry mustard - 2 teaspoons
- Onion powder - 2 teaspoons
- Cayenne pepper - 1 teaspoon
- Smoked paprika - 2 teaspoons
- Ground coffee - 2 teaspoons
- Olive oil - ¼ cup

THE SAUCE

- Bourbon - 1 ½ cups
- Brown sugar - ¾ cup
- Ketchup - ¾ cup
- Worcestershire sauce - 3 tablespoons
- Soy sauce - 1 tablespoon
- Lemon juice - 3 tablespoons
- Apple cider vinegar - ¼ cup
- Salt - a pinch
- Pepper - ¼ teaspoon
- Cayenne pepper - 1 teaspoon
- Sweet paprika - 1 teaspoon

The Heat

- Lump charcoal

- Cherry wood chips

The Water Bath

- Water – 2 cups

Method

1. Combine the rub ingredients--brown sugar, salt, dry mustard, onion powder, cayenne pepper, smoked paprika, and ground coffee. Mix well.

2. Pour olive oil into the spice mixture and stir until becoming a paste.

3. Rub the beef ribs with the spice mixture and put it into a zipper-lock plastic bag.

4. Marinate the beef ribs for at least 3 hours and store them in the fridge to keep the beef ribs fresh.

5. Prepare the Big Green Egg and fill it with lump charcoal and starters.

6. Ignite the starters and sprinkle woodchips over the lump charcoal or place the wood chips in a stainless woodchip box.

7. Set a convEGGtor or a plate setter in the Big Green Egg and put a disposable aluminum pan on it.

8. Pour water into the aluminum pan and set a grill grate on top.

9. Close the Big Green Egg with the lid and set the vent to reach 225°F (107°C).

10. Take the marinated beef ribs out of the fridge and thaw them at room temperature.

11. Wait until the Big Green Egg is ready and place the marinated beef ribs on the grate. Smoke the beef ribs for approximately 5 hours.

12. In the meantime, place the entire sauce ingredients--bourbon, brown sugar, ketchup, Worcestershire sauce, soy sauce, lemon juice, apple cider vinegar, salt, pepper, cayenne pepper, and sweet paprika in a saucepan.

13. Stir the sauce and bring it to a simmer over very low heat. Cook until the sauce is thickened.

14. Remove the sauce from heat and let it cool.

15. After that, check the internal temperature of the smoked beef ribs and once it reaches 165°F (74°C), remove the smoked beef ribs from the Big Green Egg.

16. Transfer the smoked beef ribs to a serving dish and drizzle the bourbon sauce on top.

17. Serve and enjoy.

Spicy Smoked Pulled Beef Tabasco

(Cooking Time 6 Hours 30 Minutes)

Ingredients for 10 servings

- Beef chuck (5-lb., 2.3-kg.)

THE MARINADE

- Tabasco - 3 tablespoons

- Soy sauce - ½ cup

- Worcestershire sauce - 3 tablespoons

- Brown sugar - 3 tablespoons

- Olive oil - 2 tablespoons

- Salt - 1 teaspoon

- Pepper - 1 teaspoon

THE GLAZE

- Tabasco - 3 tablespoons

- Ketchup - 1 cup

- Molasses - ½ cup

- Balsamic vinegar - ½ cup

- Brown sugar - 2 ½ tablespoon

- Salt - A pinch

THE HEAT

- Lump charcoal

- Cherry wood chips

THE WATER BATH

- Water – 2 cups

METHOD

1. Mix Tabasco with soy sauce, Worcestershire sauce, olive oil, brown sugar, salt, and pepper.

2. Rub the Tabasco mixture over the beef chuck and put the beef chucks into a zipper-lock plastic bag.

3. Marinate the beef chuck for at least 3 hours and store it in the fridge to keep the beef chuck fresh.

4. After 3 hours, take the marinated beef chuck out of the fridge and thaw it at room temperature.

5. Prepare the Big Green Egg and fill it with lump charcoal and starters.

6. Ignite the starters and sprinkle woodchips over the lump charcoal or place the wood chips in a stainless woodchip box.

7. Set a convEGGtor or a plate setter in the Big Green Egg and put a disposable aluminum pan on it.

8. Pour water into the aluminum pan and set a grill grate on top.

9. Close the Big Green Egg with the lid and set the vent to reach 225°F (107°C).

10. Wait until the Big Green Egg is ready and place the marinated beef chuck on the grate. Smoke it for 3 hours.

11. In the meantime, combine the glaze mixture--Tabasco, ketchup, molasses, balsamic vinegar, brown sugar, and salt in a bowl. Stir until incorporated.

12. After 3 hours of smoking, baste half of the glaze mixture over the beef chuck and continue smoking for 2 hours.

13. After that, baste the remaining glaze mixture over the beef chucks and wrap it with aluminum foil.

14. Return the wrapped beef chuck to the Big Green Egg and continue smoking for an hour or until the internal temperature reaches 195°F (91°C).

15. Remove the smoked beef chuck from the Big Green Egg and let it rest for 15 minutes.

16. Unwrap the smoked beef chuck and using a fork or a sharp knife shred it.

17. Transfer the pulled beef chuck to a serving dish and serve.

18. Enjoy!

COGNAC INJECTED SMOKED BEEF TENDERLOIN WITH CREAMY SAUCE

(COOKING TIME 5 HOURS 30 MINUTES)

INGREDIENTS FOR 10 SERVINGS

- Beef tenderloin (5-lb., 2.3-kg.)

THE INJECTION

- Cognac - ½ cup

- Unsalted butter, melted - ¾ cup

THE RUB

- Salt - 1 ¼ teaspoon
- Smoked paprika - ¼ cup
- Onion powder - 3 tablespoons
- Garlic powder - 3 tablespoons
- Oregano - 3 tablespoons
- Brown sugar - 1 ½ tablespoon
- Ground cumin - 1 ½ tablespoon
- Coarse black pepper - 3 tablespoons

THE SAUCE

- Unsalted butter - 2 tablespoons
- Diced shallots - 3 tablespoons
- Cognac - ½ cup
- Heavy cream - 3 cups
- Dijon mustard - 3 tablespoons
- Dried thyme - 1 teaspoon
- Salt - a pinch
- Pepper - ¼ teaspoon

THE HEAT

- Lump charcoal
- Alder wood chips

THE WATER BATH

- Water – 2 cups

METHOD

1. Combine the injection ingredients--melted butter and cognac then stir until incorporated.

2. Fill an injector with the mixture and inject it into the beef tenderloin at several places. Set aside.

3. Mix the rub ingredients--salt, smoked paprika, onion powder, garlic powder, oregano, brown sugar, cumin, and black pepper.

4. Apply the spice mixture over the injected beef tenderloin and cover it with plastic wrap.

5. Let the seasoned beef tenderloin rest for at least 5 hours or overnight and store it in the fridge to keep the beef tenderloin fresh.

6. Fill the Big Green Egg with lump charcoal and starters then ignite the starters.

7. Sprinkle wood chips over the lump charcoal or place the wood chips in a stainless woodchip box.

8. Set a convEGGtor or a plate setter in the Big Green Egg and put a disposable aluminum pan on it.

9. Pour water into the aluminum pan and set a grill grate on top.

10. Close the Big Green Egg with the lid and set the vent to reach 225°F (107°C).

11. Remove the seasoned beef brisket from the fridge and unwrap it. Thaw at room temperature.

12. Wait until the Big Green Egg is ready and place the seasoned beef tenderloin on the grate.

13. Smoke the beef tenderloin for 5 hours or until the internal temperature reaches 185°F (85°C).

14. In the meantime, make the sauce in a saucepan.

15. Melt the unsalted butter over low heat and stir in the diced shallots. Sauté until wilted.

16. Pour cognac and heavy cream into the saucepan then season it with Dijon mustard, dried thyme, salt, and pepper.

17. Bring the sauce to a simmer and stir well. Remove from heat and let it cool.

18. Once the smoked beef tenderloin is done, take it out of the Big Green Egg and transfer it to a serving dish.

19. Drizzle the creamy sauce on top and serve.

20. Enjoy!

Classic Smoked Beef Loaf with Sweet Garlic Glaze

(Cooking Time 4 Hours 10 Minutes)

Ingredients for 10 servings

- Ground beef (5-lb., 2.3-kg.)

THE SPICES

- Diced onion - 2 cups
- Bread crumbs - 1 cup
- Eggs - 4 eggs
- Fresh milk - 3 tablespoons
- Dijon mustard - 2 tablespoons
- Worcestershire sauce - ¼ cup
- Minced garlic - 3 tablespoons
- Ketchup - ½ cup
- Salt - 1 ¼ teaspoon
- Italian seasoning - 1 tablespoon
- Black pepper - ½ teaspoon
- Smoked paprika - 2 teaspoons
- Brown sugar - 2 tablespoons

THE GLAZE

- Ketchup - 1 cup
- Balsamic vinegar - 2 teaspoons
- Brown sugar - 3 tablespoons
- Garlic powder - 2 teaspoons
- Onion powder - 1 teaspoon
- Black pepper - ½ teaspoon
- Salt - A pinch

THE HEAT

- Lump charcoal

- Mixed of hickory and apple woodchips

THE WATER BATH

- Water – 2 cups

METHOD

1. Add diced onion, breadcrumbs, and eggs to the ground beef. Mix well.

2. Season the ground beef mixture with Dijon mustard, Worcestershire sauce, minced garlic, ketchup, salt, Italian seasoning, black pepper, smoked paprika, and brown sugar.

3. Pour milk into the ground beef mixture and shape it into a loaf form. Place it on a sheet of aluminum foil.

4. Next, combine the glaze ingredients--ketchup, balsamic vinegar, brown sugar, garlic powder, onion powder, black pepper, and salt. Stir until incorporated.

5. Baste the glaze mixture over the beef loaf and wrap it with aluminum foil. Set aside.

6. Prepare the Big Green Egg and fill it with lump charcoal and starters.

7. Ignite the starters and sprinkle woodchips over the lump charcoal or place the wood chips in a stainless woodchip box.

8. Set a convEGGtor or a plate setter in the Big Green Egg and put a disposable aluminum pan on it.

9. Pour water into the aluminum pan and set a grill grate on top.

10. Close the Big Green Egg with the lid and set the vent to reach 250°F (121°C).

11. Wait until the Big Green Egg is ready and place the wrapped beef loaf on the grill grate.

12. Smoke the beef loaf for 4 hours and regularly check the internal temperature.

13. Once the internal temperature of the smoked beef loaf reaches 160°F (71°C), remove it from the Big Green Egg and let it rest for approximately 30 minutes.

14. Unwrap the smoked beef loaf and cut it into thick slices.

15. Serve and enjoy.

SENSATIONAL CHILI SMOKED BEEF BRISKET WITH COCOA COFFEE RUB

(COOKING TIME 5 HOURS 30 MINUTES)

INGREDIENTS FOR 10 SERVINGS

- Beef brisket (4-lbs., 1.8-kg.)

THE INJECTION

- Brewed Coffee – 2 cups
- Brown sugar – ¾ cup

THE RUB

- Smoked Paprika – 3 tablespoons
- Onion powder – 1 ½ tablespoons
- Chili Powder – 2 teaspoons
- Garlic powder – 1 ½ tablespoons
- Mustard powder – 1 ½ teaspoons
- Ground coriander – 1 ½ teaspoons
- Oregano – 1 ½ teaspoons
- Dried thyme – 1 ½ teaspoons
- Brown sugar – 3 tablespoons
- Kosher salt – 1 ½ tablespoons
- Ground coffee – ¾ cup
- Cocoa powder – ½ cup

THE GLAZE

- Butter – ¼ cup

THE HEAT

- Lump charcoal
- Alder wood chips

The Water Bath

- Apple juice – 2 cups
- Cloves – 2

Method

1. Add brown sugar to the brewed coffee then stir until incorporated.

2. Fill the brewed coffee mixture into an injector then inject the beef brisket at several places. Set aside.

3. Combine the rub ingredients—smoked paprika, onion powder, chili powder, garlic powder, mustard powder, ground coriander, oregano, dried thyme, brown sugar, kosher salt, ground coffee, and cocoa in a bowl then stir well.

4. Rub the beef brisket with the spice mixture then cover with plastic wrap. Let it rest for at least 5 hours or overnight and store in the fridge to keep it fresh.

5. Fill the Big Green Egg with lump charcoal and starters then ignite the starters.

6. Sprinkle wood chips over the lump charcoal or place the wood chips in a stainless woodchip box.

7. Set a convEGGtor or a plate setter in the Big Green Egg and put a disposable aluminum pan on it.

8. Pour apple juice and add cloves to the aluminum pan then set a grill grate on top.

9. Close the Big Green Egg with the lid and set the vent to reach 225°F (107°C).

10. Remove the seasoned beef brisket from the fridge and unwrap it. Thaw at room temperature.

11. Once the Big Green Egg is ready, place the seasoned beef brisket on the grate and smoke for 5 hours or until the internal temperature of the smoked beef brisket has reached 185°F (85°C).

12. Remove the smoked beef brisket from the Big Green Egg and quickly baste butter over the smoked beef brisket.

13. Wrap the smoked beef brisket and let it sit for approximately 30 minutes.

14. Unwrap the smoked beef brisket and cut into slices.

15. Serve and enjoy!

Chapter-2 PORK

Sticky Sweet Soy Glazed Smoked Pork Ribs with Gingery Marinade

(Cooking Time 5 Hours 10 Minutes)

Ingredients for 10 servings

- Baby back ribs (7-lb., 3.175-kg.)

The Marinade

- Grated ginger - 1 tablespoon
- Sesame oil - 1 tablespoon
- Onion powder - 2 teaspoons
- Garlic powder - 2 teaspoons
- Brown sugar - 2 tablespoons
- Rice wine vinegar - 3 tablespoons
- Honey - ¼ cup
- Chili powder - 2 teaspoons
- Olive oil - ½ cup
- Soy sauce - 1 ½ cups

The Glaze

- Soy sauce - ¼ cup
- Honey - 3 tablespoons
- White vinegar - ¼ cup
- Brown sugar - ¾ cup
- Sesame oil - 1 tablespoon
- Grated ginger - ½ teaspoon
- Garlic powder - ½ teaspoon
- Salt - A pinch

THE HEAT

- Lump charcoal

- Alder wood chips

THE WATER BATH

- Water – 2 cups

METHOD

1. Combine the marinade ingredients--grated ginger, sesame oil, onion powder, garlic powder, brown sugar, rice wine vinegar, honey, chili powder, chili powder, olive oil, and soy sauce. Mix well.

2. Rub the seasoning mixture over the baby back ribs and marinate the ribs for at least 6 hours or overnight. Store the marinated baby back ribs in the fridge to keep them fresh.

3. On the next day, take the marinated baby back ribs out of the fridge and thaw them at room temperature.

1. In the meantime, prepare the Big Green Egg and fill it with lump charcoal and starters.

4. Ignite the starters and sprinkle wood chips over the lump charcoal or place the wood chips in a stainless woodchip box.

5. Set a convEGGtor or a plate setter in the Big Green Egg and put a disposable aluminum pan on it.

6. Pour water into the aluminum pan and set a grill grate on top.

7. Close the Big Green Egg with the lid and set the vent to reach 225°F (107°C).

8. Arrange the marinated baby back ribs on the grill grate inside the Big Green Egg and smoke them for 3 hours.

9. In the meantime, place the soy sauce, honey, and white vinegar in a saucepan and stir well.

10. Add brown sugar, sesame oil, grated ginger, garlic powder, and salt to the saucepan and bring it to a simmer over low heat. Stir until incorporated.

11. Remove the sauce from heat and let it cool.

12. After 3 hours of smoking, take the baby back ribs out of the Big Green Egg and arrange them on a sheet of aluminum foil.

13. Baste the glaze mixture over the baby back ribs and wrap them with aluminum foil.

14. Return the wrapped baby back ribs to the Big Green Egg and continue smoking for another 2 hours.

15. Once the internal temperature of the smoked baby back ribs reaches 145°F (63°C), remove them from the Big Green Egg and let them rest for 30 minutes.

16. Unwrap the smoked baby back ribs and transfer them to a serving dish.

17. Serve and enjoy!

LIGHT CAYENNE GLAZED SMOKED PORK SHANK WITH SWEET MAPLE MARINADE

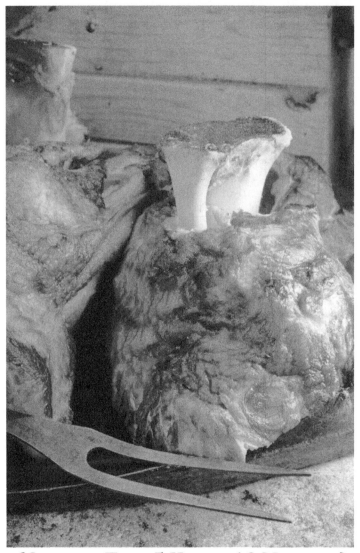

(COOKING TIME 5 HOURS 10 MINUTES)

INGREDIENTS FOR 10 SERVINGS

- Pork shank (6-lb., 2.7-kg.)

The Marinade

- Maple syrup - ½ cup

- Red wine vinegar - ½ cup

- Dijon mustard - ½ cup

- Olive oil - ½ cup

The Rub

- Brown sugar - 3 tablespoons

- Smoked paprika - ¼ cup

- Salt - 1 ½ teaspoon

- Garlic powder - 2 tablespoons

- Onion powder - 1 tablespoon

- Pepper - 1 teaspoon

- Chili powder - 1 tablespoon

- Chipotle chili powder - 1 tablespoon

- Cayenne pepper - 1 teaspoon

- Cumin - ½ tablespoon

- Dry mustard - 1 teaspoon

THE GLAZE

- Butter - 2 tablespoons

- Balsamic vinegar - 3 tablespoons

- Brown sugar - ½ cup

- Garlic powder - ½ teaspoon

THE SAUCE

- Apple cider vinegar - 1 cup

- Chicken broth - ¾ cup

- Brown sugar - ½ cup

- Ketchup - 2 tablespoons

- Worcestershire sauce - 2 tablespoons

- Garlic powder - ½ teaspoon

- Onion powder - ½ teaspoon

- Smoked paprika - ½ teaspoon

- Salt - A pinch

- Pepper - ¼ teaspoon

- Cayenne pepper - ½ teaspoon

- Red chili flakes - ½ teaspoon

- Diced parsley - 2 teaspoons

THE HEAT

- Lump charcoal
- Alder wood chips

THE WATER BATH

- Water – 2 cups

METHOD

1. Pour maple syrup, red wine vinegar, olive oil, and Dijon mustard in a container. Mix well.

2. Rub the pork shank with the mixture and marinate it for at least 4 hours or overnight. Store the marinated pork shank in the fridge to keep the pork shank fresh.

3. On the next day, take the marinated pork shank out of the fridge and thaw it at room temperature.

4. In the meantime, combine the rub ingredients--brown sugar, smoked paprika, salt, garlic powder, onion powder, pepper, chili powder, chipotle chili powder, cayenne pepper, cumin, and dry mustard.

5. Apply the rub mixture over the pork shank and set aside.

6. Next, prepare the Big Green Egg and fill it with lump charcoal and starters.

7. Ignite the starters and sprinkle wood chips over the lump charcoal or place the wood chips in a stainless woodchip box.

8. Set a convEGGtor or a plate setter in the Big Green Egg and put a disposable aluminum pan on it.

9. Pour water into the aluminum pan and set a grill grate on top.

10. Close the Big Green Egg with the lid and set the vent to reach 225°F (107°C).

11. Wait until the Big Green Egg is ready and place the seasoned pork shank on the grill grate inside the Big Green Egg. Smoke the pork shank for 2 hours.

12. Meanwhile, melt the butter over low heat.

13. Add balsamic vinegar, brown sugar, and garlic powder to the melted butter. Stir until incorporated.

14. After 2 hours of smoking, baste the pork shank with the glaze mixture and arrange the pork shank in a disposable aluminum pan.

15. Return the pork shank to the Big Green Egg and continue smoking for 3 hours.

16. While waiting for the smoked pork shank, pour apple cider vinegar and chicken broth into a saucepan.

17. Add brown sugar, ketchup, and Worcestershire sauce to the saucepan and season the sauce with the remaining ingredients-- garlic powder, onion powder, smoked paprika, salt, pepper, cayenne pepper, and red chili flakes.

18. Stir the sauce until incorporated and bring it to a simmer over low heat. Remove from heat and let it cool.

19. Regularly check the internal temperature of the smoked pork shank. Once it reaches 170°F (77°C), remove the smoked pork shank from the Big Green Egg.

20. Place the smoked pork shank on a serving dish and drizzle the sauce over it.

21. Sprinkle diced parsley on top and serve.

22. Enjoy!

SMOKED PORK TENDERLOIN WITH REFRESHING CITRUS AND CILANTRO AROMA

(COOKING TIME 5 HOURS 10 MINUTES)

INGREDIENTS FOR 10 SERVINGS

- Pork tenderloin (4-lbs., 1.8-kg.)

THE MARINADE

- Orange juice - 1 cup
- Lemon juice - ¾ cup
- Olive oil - ¼ cup
- Ground cumin - 1 tablespoon
- Chili powder - 2 teaspoons
- Salt - 1 teaspoon
- Dried oregano - 1 teaspoon
- Black pepper - 1 teaspoon
- Garlic powder - 1 teaspoon
- Chopped fresh cilantro - ¾ cup

THE RUB

- Navel oranges - ½ lb.
- Orange juice - ½ cup
- Vegetable oil - ¼ cup
- Sweet paprika - ¼ cup
- Cayenne pepper - 2 teaspoons
- Minced garlic - ¼ cup
- Salt - 1 teaspoon

The Heat

- Lump charcoal

- Cherry wood chips

The Water Bath

- Water – 2 cups

Method

1. Combine the marinade ingredients in a container.

2. Pour orange juice, lemon juice, and olive oil into the container.

3. Season the marinade mixture with cumin, chili powder, salt, oregano, black pepper, and garlic powder. Stir until incorporated.

4. Add chopped fresh cilantro to the marinade mixture and mix well.

5. Score the pork tenderloin at several places and rub the tenderloin with the cilantro mixture.

6. Marinate the pork tenderloin for at least 4 hours or overnight and store it in the fridge to keep the pork tenderloin fresh.

7. On the next day, take the marinated pork tenderloin out of the fridge and thaw it at room temperature.

8. In the meantime, cut the navel orange into quarters and place them in a food processor.

9. Add orange juice, vegetable oil, sweet paprika, cayenne pepper, minced garlic, and salt to the food processor. Process until becoming a paste.

10. Apply the seasoning paste over the pork tenderloin and set aside.

11. Next, prepare the Big Green Egg and fill it with lump charcoal and starters.

12. Ignite the starters and sprinkle wood chips over the lump charcoal or place the wood chips in a stainless woodchip box.

13. Set a convEGGtor or a plate setter in the Big Green Egg and put a disposable aluminum pan on it.

14. Pour water into the aluminum pan and set a grill grate on top.

15. Close the Big Green Egg with the lid and set the vent to reach 225°F (107°C).

16. Place the seasoned pork tenderloin on the grill grate inside the Big Green Egg and smoke it for 5 hours.

17. Once the internal temperature reaches 160°F (71°C), remove the smoked pork tenderloin from the Big Green Egg and transfer it to a serving dish.

18. Cut the smoked pork tenderloin into thick slices and serve.

19. Enjoy!

GINGER BEER MARINADE SMOKED PORK BUTT WITH APRICOT GLAZE

(COOKING TIME 6 HOURS 10 MINUTES)

INGREDIENTS FOR 10 SERVINGS

- Pork butt (5-lb., 2.3-kg.)

THE MARINADE

- Ginger beer - 3 cups
- Apple cider vinegar - ¼ cup
- Black peppercorns - 1 ½ tablespoon
- Brown sugar - 3 tablespoons
- Salt - 1 ¼ teaspoon

THE GLAZE

- Ginger beer - 3 cups
- Ketchup ½ cup
- Apricot jam - 1.2 cup
- Honey - 1 tablespoon
- Soy sauce - 1 tablespoon
- Apple cider vinegar - 2 tablespoons
- Worcestershire sauce - 1 tablespoon
- Garlic powder - 2 teaspoons

THE HEAT

- Lump charcoal
- Mixed of Alder and Cherry wood chips

THE WATER BATH

- Water – 2 cups

METHOD

1. Combine ginger beer with apple cider vinegar, black peppercorns, brown sugar, and salt. Stir well.

2. Score the pork butt at several places and rub it with the spice mixture.

3. Marinate the pork butt overnight and store it in the fridge to keep the pork butt fresh.

4. On the next day, take the marinated pork butt out of the fridge and thaw it at room temperature.

5. Next, prepare the Big Green Egg and fill it with lump charcoal and starters.

6. Ignite the starters and sprinkle wood chips over the lump charcoal or place the wood chips in a stainless woodchip box.

7. Set a convEGGtor or a plate setter in the Big Green Egg and put a disposable aluminum pan on it.

8. Pour water into the aluminum pan and set a grill grate on top.

9. Close the Big Green Egg with the lid and set the vent to reach 225°F (107°C).

10. Wait until the Big Green Egg reaches the desired temperature and place the marinated pork butt on the grill grate inside the Big Green Egg. Smoke the pork butt for 3 hours.

11. In the meantime, pour ginger beer into a saucepan together with ketchup, apricot jam, honey, soy sauce, apple cider vinegar, Worcestershire sauce, and garlic powder.

12. Stir the glaze mixture well and bring it to simmer. Cook the glaze mixture until it is thickened and remove it from heat.

13. After 3 hours of smoking, take the pork butt out of the Big Green Egg and transfer it to a disposable aluminum pan.

14. Spread then glaze mixture over the pork butt and cover it with aluminum foil.

15. Return the pork butt to the Big Green Egg and smoke it for another 3 hours.

16. Once the internal temperature reaches 170°F (77°C), remove the smoked pork butt from the Big Green Egg.

17. Let the smoked pork butt rest for approximately 15 minutes and unwrap it.

18. Serve and enjoy!

Sweet Rub Smoked Pork Belly with Apple Ginger BBQ Glaze

(Cooking Time 6 Hours 10 Minutes)

Ingredients for 10 servings

- Pork Belly (4-lbs., 1.8-kg.)

The Rub

- Kosher salt – 1 tablespoon

- Brown sugar – ¼ cup

- Granulated sugar – 3 tablespoons

- Smoked paprika – 2 tablespoons

- Garlic powder – 2 teaspoons

- Pepper – 1 teaspoon

- Mustard – 1 teaspoon

The Glaze

- Apple juice – ½ cup

- Ginger – 2 teaspoons

- Vegetable oil – 2 tablespoons

- Chili powder – ¼ teaspoon

- Ketchup – 1 cup

- Oyster sauce – 2 tablespoons

- Apple cider vinegar – 2 tablespoons

- Mustard – ½ teaspoon

The Heat

- Lump charcoal
- Mixed of Cherry and Pear

The Water Bath

- Apple juice – 2 cups
- Cloves – 2

Method

1. Prepare the Big Green Egg then fill it with lump charcoal and starters. Ignite the starters.

2. Sprinkle wood chips over the lump charcoal or place the wood chips in a stainless woodchip box.

3. Set a convEGGtor or a plate setter in the Big Green Egg and place a disposable aluminum pan on it.

4. Pour apple juice into the aluminum pan then add cloves into it.

5. After that, set a grill grate on top then close the Big Green Egg with the lid. Set the vent to reach 200°F (93°C).

6. While waiting for the Big Green Egg reaches the desired temperature, combine the rub ingredients—kosher salt, brown sugar, granulated sugar, smoked paprika, garlic powder, pepper, and mustard then mix well.

7. Cut the pork belly into medium cubes then rub with the spice mixture.

8. Once the Big Green Egg is ready, arrange the seasoned pork belly cubes on the grill grate inside the Big Green Egg and smoke for 3 hours.

9. In the meantime, combine apple juice with ginger, vegetable oil, chili powder, ketchup, oyster sauce, apple cider vinegar, and mustard then stir until incorporated.

10. After 3 hours of smoking, remove the pork belly from the Big Green Egg and transfer to a disposable aluminum pan.

11. Drizzle the glaze mixture over the pork belly cubes then toss to coat.

12. Return the pork belly to the Big Green Egg and continue smoking for another 3 hours or until the internal temperature of the smoked pork belly has reached 165°F (74°C).

13. Once it is done, remove from the Big Green Egg and transfer the smoked pork belly to a serving dish.

14. Serve and enjoy!

CHAPTER-3 HAM

CHILI CAYENNE SMOKED HAM WITH WALNUT AND PECAN AROMA

(COOKING TIME 2 HOURS 10 MINUTES)

INGREDIENTS FOR 10 SERVINGS

- Ham (4-lbs., 1.8-kg.)

THE MARINADE

- Salt - ½ teaspoon
- Black pepper - 2 teaspoons
- Garlic powder - 1 tablespoon
- Onion powder - 2 teaspoons
- Smoked paprika - 1 tablespoon
- Dried rosemary - 2 teaspoons
- Cayenne pepper - 1 pepper
- Dijon mustard - 1 teaspoon
- Red wine vinegar - ½ cup

THE RUB

- Smoked paprika - 1 tablespoon
- Salt - 1 teaspoon
- Garlic powder - 1 tablespoon
- Onion powder - 1 tablespoon
- Black pepper - 1 teaspoon
- Cayenne pepper - 1 tablespoon
- Chili powder - ½ teaspoon
- Oregano - 1 teaspoon
- Ground cumin - ½ teaspoon
- Coriander - 2 teaspoons

THE HEAT

- Lump charcoal

- Mixed of pecan and walnut woodchips

THE WATER BATH

- Water – 2 cups

METHOD

1. Combine salt with black pepper, garlic powder, onion powder, smoked paprika, dried rosemary, cayenne pepper, and Dijon mustard.

2. Pour red wine vinegar over the spice mixture and mix until becoming a paste.

3. Rub the ham with the spice mixture and wrap it with plastic wrap.

4. Marinate the ham for at least 8 hours or overnight and store it in the fridge to make the ham fresh.

5. On the next day, take the marinated ham out of the fridge and thaw it at room temperature.

6. Combine the rub ingredients--smoked paprika, salt, garlic powder, onion powder, black pepper, cayenne pepper, chili powder, oregano, ground cumin, and coriander.

7. Apply the spice mixture over the ham and set aside.

8. Prepare the Big Green Egg and fill it with lump charcoal and starters.

9. Ignite the starters and sprinkle woodchips over the lump charcoal or place the wood chips in a stainless woodchip box.

10. Set a convEGGtor or a plate setter in the Big Green Egg and put a disposable aluminum pan on it.

11. Pour water into the aluminum pan and set a grill grate on top.

12. Close the Big Green Egg with the lid and set the vent to reach 225°F (107°C).

13. Place the seasoned ham on the grate and smoke it for 2 hours.

14. Once the internal temperature of the smoked ham reaches 140°F (60°C), remove it from the Big Green Egg.

15. Quickly wrap the smoked ham and let it rest for approximately 30 minutes.

16. Unwrap the smoked ham and cut it into slices.

17. Serve and enjoy.

Aromatic Lemon Rub Smoked Ham with Honey Glaze

(COOKING TIME 3 HOURS 10 MINUTES)

INGREDIENTS FOR 10 SERVINGS

- Ham (5-lb., 2.3-kg.)

THE RUB

- Lemon juice - ¼ cup

- Grated lemon zest - 1 teaspoon

- Minced shallot - ½ teaspoon

- Olive oil - 1 tablespoon

- White wine - ½ cup

- Salt - 1 ¼ teaspoon

- Pepper - ½ teaspoon

THE GLAZE

- Honey - 6 tablespoons

- Butter - 6 tablespoon

THE HEAT

- Lump charcoal

- Mixed of Alder and Cherry wood chips

THE WATER BATH

- Water – 2 cups

METHOD

1. Score the ham at several places and rub it with lemon juice, grated lemon zest, minced shallot, olive oil, white wine, salt, and pepper.

2. Wrap the seasoned ham with plastic wrap and let it rest for at least 6 hours or overnight. Store the seasoned ham in the fridge to keep it fresh.

3. On the next day, take the seasoned ham out of the fridge and unwrap it. Thaw it at room temperature.

4. Next, prepare the Big Green Egg and fill it with lump charcoal and starters.

5. Ignite the starters and sprinkle wood chips over the lump charcoal or place the wood chips in a stainless woodchip box.

6. Set a convEGGtor or a plate setter in the Big Green Egg and put a disposable aluminum pan on it.

7. Pour water into the aluminum pan and set a grill grate on top.

8. Close the Big Green Egg with the lid and set the vent to reach 225°F (107°C).

9. Wait until the Big Green Egg is ready and place the seasoned ham on the grill inside the Big Green Egg.

10. Smoke the ham for 6 hours and regularly baste butter over the ham.

11. Once the internal temperature of the smoked ham reaches 170°F (77°C), remove it from the Big Green Egg.

12. Place the smoked ham on a serving dish and baste honey over it.

13. Serve and enjoy.

White Wine and Lemon Smoked Ham with Herbs Rub

(Cooking Time 2 Hours 30 Minutes)

Ingredients for 10 servings

- Ham (4-lbs., 1.8-kg.)

THE MARINADE

- Minced garlic - 2 tablespoons
- Lemon juice - ¼ cup
- White wine - ¾ cup
- Olive oil - 3 tablespoons
- Mustard powder - 2 tablespoons
- Honey - ¼ cup
- Thyme - 1 teaspoon
- Kosher salt - ¼ teaspoon

THE RUB

- Minced garlic - 3 tablespoons
- Minced fresh rosemary - 1 tablespoon
- Minced fresh thyme - 1 tablespoon
- Brown sugar - 3 tablespoons
- Salt - 1 ¼ teaspoon
- Black pepper - 1 teaspoon
- Cayenne pepper - ½ teaspoon
- Grated lemon zest - 1 teaspoon
- Lemon juice - 2 tablespoons
- Olive oil - 3 tablespoons

THE HEAT

- Lump charcoal

- Mixed of Apple and Oak wood chips

THE WATER BATH

- Apple juice - 1 cup

- Water - 1 cup

METHOD

1. Combine the marinade ingredients in a container.

2. Add minced garlic to the lemon juice, white wine, olive oil, mustard powder, honey, thyme, and salt. Mix well.

3. Score the ham at several places and apply the marinade mixture over it.

4. Marinate the ham leg for at least 6 hours or overnight and store it in a fridge to keep the ham fresh.

5. On the next day, take the marinated ham out of the fridge and thaw it at room temperature.

6. Next, combine the rub ingredients--minced garlic, rosemary, thyme, brown sugar, salt, black pepper, cayenne pepper, grated lemon zest, lemon juice, and olive oil. Mix until becoming a paste.

7. Rub the marinated ham with the seasoning paste and set aside.

8. Prepare the Big Green Egg and fill it with lump charcoal and starters.

9. Ignite the starters and sprinkle wood chips over the lump charcoal or place the wood chips in a stainless woodchip box.

10. Set a convEGGtor or a plate setter in the Big Green Egg and put a disposable aluminum pan on it.

11. Pour apple juice and water into the aluminum pan and set a grill grate on top.

12. Close the Big Green Egg with the lid and set the vent to reach 250°F (121°C).

13. Wait until the Big Green Egg is ready and place the seasoned ham on the grill grate inside the Big Green Egg.

14. Smoke the ham for approximately 2 hours or until the internal temperature of the ham leg reaches 140°F (60°C).

15. Remove the smoked ham from the Big Green Egg and quickly wrap it with aluminum foil.

16. Let the smoked ham rest for approximately 30 minutes and unwrap it.

17. Cut the smoked ham into slices and serve.

18. Enjoy!

BLACK COFFEE RUB SMOKED HAM WITH CHILI AND CAYENNE PEPPER

(COOKING TIME 2 HOURS 30 MINUTES)

INGREDIENTS FOR 10 SERVINGS

- Ham (4-lbs., 1.8-kg.)

THE RUB

- Ground coffee - 3 tablespoons

- Cayenne pepper - ½ teaspoon

- Chili powder - 1 tablespoon

- Ground cumin - 1 ½ teaspoon

- Ground coriander - ¾ teaspoon

- Garlic powder - 2 teaspoons

- Mustard powder - 1 teaspoon

- Salt - 1 teaspoon

THE HEAT

- Lump charcoal

- Mixed of Apple and Oak wood chips

THE WATER BATH

- Brewed coffee - 2 cups

METHOD

1. Combine ground coffee with cayenne pepper, chili powder, cumin, coriander, garlic powder, mustard powder, and salt. Mix well.

2. Score the ham at several places and apply the seasoning over it.

3. Next, prepare the Big Green Egg and fill it with lump charcoal and starters.

4. Ignite the starters and sprinkle wood chips over the lump charcoal or place the wood chips in a stainless woodchip box.

5. Set a convEGGtor or a plate setter in the Big Green Egg and put a disposable aluminum pan on it.

6. Pour brewed into the aluminum pan and set a grill grate on top.

7. Close the Big Green Egg with the lid and set the vent to reach 250°F (121°C).

8. Wait until the Big Green Egg is ready and place the seasoned ham on the grill grate inside the Big Green Egg.

9. Smoke the seasoned ham for 2 hours or until the internal temperature reaches 140°F (60°C).

10. Once it is done, remove the smoked ham from the Big Green Egg and wrap it with aluminum foil.

11. Let the wrapped smoked ham for 30 minutes and unwrap it.

12. Serve and enjoy!

CHAPTER-4 LAMB

INJECTION SMOKED LAMB SHOULDER WITH ROASTED GARLIC AND ORANGE INJECTION

(Cooking Time 5 Hours 10 Minutes)

Ingredients for 10 servings

- Lamb shoulder (5-lb., 2.3-kg.)

The Injection

- Roasted garlic - 2 heads

- Orange juice - 1 cup

- Mustard powder - 2 tablespoons

- Honey - ¼ cup

- Thyme - 1 teaspoon

The Rub

- Minced garlic - 3 tablespoons

- Minced rosemary - 1 tablespoon

- Minced thyme - 1 tablespoon

- Salt - 1 ¼ teaspoon

- Black pepper - 1 teaspoon

- Olive oil - ¼ cup

The Spray

- Garlic cloves - 3

- Water - 1 cup

The Heat

- Lump charcoal

- Mixed of Alder and Cherry wood chips

The Water Bath

- Water – 2 cups

Method

1. Place roasted garlic together with orange juice, mustard powder, honey, and thyme in a blender. Blend until incorporated.

2. Fill an injector with the mixture and inject it into the lamb shoulder at several places. Set aside.

3. Next, combine the rub ingredients--minced garlic, rosemary, thyme, salt, and black pepper.

4. Pour olive oil over the mixture and mix it until becoming a paste.

5. Rub the lamb shoulder with the seasoning mixture and set aside.

6. After that, prepare the Big Green Egg and fill it with lump charcoal and starters.

7. Ignite the starters and sprinkle wood chips over the lump charcoal or place the wood chips in a stainless woodchip box.

8. Set a convEGGtor or a plate setter in the Big Green Egg and put a disposable aluminum pan on it.

9. Pour water into the aluminum pan and set a grill grate on top.

10. Close the Big Green Egg with the lid and set the vent to reach 225°F (107°C).

11. While waiting for the Big Green Egg to get ready, blend garlic cloves with water and strain it completely.

12. Pour the liquid mixture into a spray bottle and set it aside.

13. When the Big Green Egg is ready, arrange the lamb shoulder on the grill grate inside the Big Green Egg and smoke it for 5 hours.

14. Regularly spray the garlic water over the lamb shoulder and continue smoking until the internal temperature of the smoked lamb shoulder reaches 135°F (57°C).

15. Remove the smoked lamb shoulder from the Big Green Egg and transfer it to a serving dish.

16. Serve and enjoy.

Honey Glazed Smoked Lamb Chops with Minty Walnut Parsley Pesto

(Cooking Time 4 Hours 30 Minutes)

Ingredients for 10 servings

- Bone in lamb chops (5-lb., 2.3-kg.)

The Rub

- Brown sugar - ½ cup

- Ground cinnamon - 1 ½ teaspoon

- Garlic powder - 1 teaspoon

- Salt - 1 ¼ teaspoon

- Pepper - 2 teaspoons

THE GLAZE

- Honey - 3 tablespoons
- Soy sauce - 2 tablespoon
- Garlic powder - ½ teaspoon
- Pepper - ½ teaspoon
- Salt - A pinch

THE SAUCE

- Toasted walnut crumbles - ½ cup
- Diced fresh parsley - 1 ½ cup
- Diced mint - 1 tablespoon
- Diced basil - 1 tablespoon
- Diced shallot - 1 tablespoon
- Minced garlic - 1 tablespoon
- Lemon juice - 2 tablespoon
- Grated lemon zest - ½ teaspoon
- Salt - A pinch
- Black pepper - ¼ teaspoon
- Walnut oil - ½ cup

THE HEAT

- Lump charcoal

- Mixed of Apple and Oak wood chips

THE WATER BATH

- Water - 1 cup

- Fresh mint leaves - 10 leaves

METHOD

1. Place the entire sauce ingredients--walnut crumbles, parsley, mint, basil, shallots, garlic, lemon juice, lemon zest, salt, and black pepper in a blender.

2. Pour the walnut oil into the blender and blend until smooth and creamy. Store the sauce in the fridge.

3. Score the lamb chop at several places and set aside.

4. Combine the rub ingredients--brown sugar, ground cinnamon, garlic powder, salt, and pepper. Mix well.

5. Apply the rub ingredients over the lamb chops and set aside.

6. Next, prepare the Big Green Egg and fill it with lump charcoal and starters.

7. Ignite the starters and sprinkle wood chips over the lump charcoal or place the wood chips in a stainless woodchip box.

8. Set a convEGGtor or a plate setter in the Big Green Egg and put a disposable aluminum pan on it.

9. Pour water and add mint leaves to the aluminum pan and set a grill grate on top.

10. Close the Big Green Egg with the lid and set the vent to reach 225°F (107°C).

11. Once the Big Green Egg is ready, place the seasoned lamb chops on the grill grate inside the Big Green Egg and smoke it for 4 hours.

12. In the meantime, combine honey with soy sauce in a bowl and stir well.

13. Season the honey and soy mixture with salt, pepper, and garlic then stir until incorporated.

14. After 4 hours of smoking, baste the glaze mixture over the lamb chops and continue smoking for another 30 minutes.

15. Check the internal temperature of the smoked lamb chops and once it reaches 165°F (74°C), remove it from the Big Green Egg.

16. Transfer the smoked lamb chop to a serving dish and drizzle the parsley sauce on top.

17. Serve and enjoy.

Sweet Ginger Smoked Lamb Ribs with Salted Butter Glaze

(Cooking Time 4 Hours 30 Minutes)

Ingredients for 10 servings

- Lamb ribs (6-lb., 2.7-kg.)

THE RUB

- Brown sugar - ¼ cup

- Ginger powder - ½ teaspoon

- Garlic powder - 1 tablespoon

- Salt - 1 ½ teaspoon

- Black pepper - 2 teaspoons

- Diced thyme - ½ teaspoon

- Sage - ½ teaspoon

- Marjoram - ½ teaspoon

- Soy sauce - 3 tablespoons

- Olive oil - 3 tablespoons

THE GLAZE

- Salted butter - 3 tablespoons

THE HEAT

- Lump charcoal

- Mixed of Cherry and Oak wood chips

THE WATER BATH

- Water - 2 cups

METHOD

1. Place brown sugar, ginger powder, garlic powder, salt, black pepper, thyme, sage, and marjoram in a bowl. Mix well.

2. Pour soy sauce and olive oil into the spice mixture and mix until becoming a paste.

3. Rub the lamb ribs with the spice mixture and let it rest for approximately an hour.

4. Next, prepare the Big Green Egg and fill it with lump charcoal and starters.

5. Ignite the starters and sprinkle wood chips over the lump charcoal or place the wood chips in a stainless woodchip box.

6. Set a convEGGtor or a plate setter in the Big Green Egg and put a disposable aluminum pan on it.

7. Pour water to the aluminum pan and set a grill grate on top.

8. Close the Big Green Egg with the lid and set the vent to reach 225°F (107°C).

9. Wait until the Big Green Egg is ready and place the seasoned lamb ribs on the grill grate inside the Big Green Egg.

10. Smoke the lamb ribs for 4 hours or until the internal temperature reaches 145°F (63°C) and remove it from the Big Green Egg.

11. Quickly baste butter over the smoked lamb ribs and place it on a sheet of aluminum foil.

12. Wrap the smoked lamb ribs with the aluminum foil and let them rest for approximately 30 minutes.

13. Unwrap the smoked lamb ribs and transfer them to a serving dish.

14. Serve and enjoy.

CINNAMON SMOKED PULLED LAMB WITH POMEGRANATE AND HONEY SAUCE

(COOKING TIME 5 HOURS 10 MINUTES)

INGREDIENTS FOR 10 SERVINGS

- Lamb shoulder (5-lb., 2.3-kg.)

THE RUB

- Brown sugar - ¼ cup

- Minced garlic - 2 tablespoons

- Ground cinnamon - 2 teaspoons

- Ground cumin - 1 teaspoon

- Oregano - 1 teaspoon

- Grated lemon zest - 1 teaspoon

- Lemon juice - 3 tablespoons

THE SPRAY

- Apple cider vinegar - ½ cup

- Apple juice - ½ cup

THE SAUCE

- Pomegranate juice - 2 cups

- Honey - 2 tablespoons

- Greek yogurt - ½ cup

- Chopped mint leaves - 1 tablespoon

THE HEAT

- Lump charcoal

- Mixed of Cherry and Oak wood chips

The Water Bath

- Water - 2 cups

Method

1. Combine brown sugar with minced garlic, ground cinnamon, cumin, oregano, and grated lemon zest. Mix well.

2. Drizzle lemon juice over the spice mixture and mix until becoming a paste. Add a little amount of water if it is necessary.

3. Rub the lamb shoulder with the spice paste and set aside.

4. Next, prepare the Big Green Egg and fill it with lump charcoal and starters.

5. Ignite the starters and sprinkle wood chips over the lump charcoal or place the wood chips in a stainless woodchip box.

6. Set a convEGGtor or a plate setter in the Big Green Egg and put a disposable aluminum pan on it.

7. Pour water to the aluminum pan and set a grill grate on top.

8. Close the Big Green Egg with the lid and set the vent to reach 225°F (107°C).

9. While waiting for the Big Green Egg gets ready, combine the apple cider vinegar with apple juice and pour the mixture into a spray bottle.

10. Once the Big Green Egg reached the desired temperature, place the seasoned lamb shoulder on the grill grate inside the Big Green Egg.

11. Smoke the lamb shoulder for 4 hours and spray the apple juice mixture over it once every 30 minutes.

12. In the meantime, pour the pomegranate juice together with honey and yogurt into a saucepan and bring it to a simmer.

13. Add diced mint leaves to the sauce mixture and cook until it is thickened.

14. Remove the sauce from heat and let it cool.

15. After 4 hours of smoking, take the smoked lamb shoulder out if the Big Green Egg. The internal temperature of the smoked lamb shoulder will be approximately 165°F (74°C).

16. Transfer the smoked lamb shoulder to a disposable aluminum pan and drizzle the pomegranate sauce over it.

17. Return the aluminum pan with smoked lamb shoulder to the Big Green Egg and continue smoking for an hour.

18. Once the internal temperature of the smoked lamb shoulder reaches 195°F (91°C), remove it from the Big Green Egg.

19. Transfer the smoked lamb shoulder to a flat surface and using a fork or a sharp knife shred the smoked lamb shoulder.

20. Place the pulled smoked lamb shoulder on a serving dish and drizzle the remaining sauce on top.

21. Serve and enjoy!

Chapter-5 POULTRY CHICKEN

Lemon Marinade Smoked Chicken Thigh with Brown Sugar Soy Dip

(Cooking Time 3 Hours 30 Minutes)

INGREDIENTS FOR 10 SERVINGS

- Chicken thighs (4-lbs., 1.8-kg.)

THE MARINADE

- Lemon juice - ¼ cup
- Grated lemon zest - 1 tablespoon
- Olive oil - 3 tablespoons
- Dijon mustard - 2 tablespoons
- Salt - ¼ teaspoon
- Pepper - 1 teaspoon
- Red chili - ½ teaspoon
- Minced garlic - 2 tablespoons
- Chopped fresh dill - 1 tablespoon
- Chopped fresh parsley - 1 tablespoon
- Chopped fresh cilantro - 1 tablespoon
- Chopped fresh basil - 1 tablespoon

THE GLAZE

- Ketchup - ¾ cup
- Brown sugar - ½ cup
- Soy sauce - ¼ cup
- Honey - 1 tablespoon
- Apple cider vinegar - 3 tablespoons
- Olive oil - 3 tablespoons
- Worcestershire sauce - 2 tablespoons
- Minced garlic - 1 tablespoon

THE HEAT

- Lump charcoal

- Mix of Alder and Apple wood chips

THE WATER BATH

- Water – 2 cups

- Lemon juice - 3 tablespoons

METHOD

1. Combine lemon juice with olive oil in a container. Mix well.

2. Season the mixture with grated lemon zest, Dijon mustard, salt, pepper, red chili, minced garlic, dill, parsley, basil, and cilantro. Stir until combined.

3. Next, rub the seasoning mixture over the chicken thighs and marinate them for at least 4 hours or overnight.

4. Store the marinated chicken thighs in the fridge to keep them fresh.

5. On the next day, take the marinated chicken thighs out of the fridge and thaw them at room temperature.

6. In the meantime, fill the Big Green Egg with lump charcoal and starters then ignite the starters.

7. Sprinkle wood chips over the lump charcoal or place the wood chips in a stainless woodchip box.

8. Set a convEGGtor or a plate setter in the Big Green Egg and put a disposable aluminum pan on it.

9. Pour water and lemon juice into the aluminum pan and set a grill grate on top.

10. Close the Big Green Egg with the lid and set the vent to reach 275°F (135°C).

11. Wait until the Big Green Egg is ready and arrange the marinated chicken thighs on the grill grate.

12. Smoke the chicken thighs for 3 hours until the internal temperature reaches 145°F (63°C).

13. Meanwhile, combine ketchup, brown sugar, soy sauce, honey, apple cider vinegar, olive oil, Worcestershire sauce, and minced garlic in a saucepan. Stir well and bring it to a simmer.

14. After 2 hours of smoking, take the smoked chicken thighs out of the Big Green Egg and dip them in the glaze mixture.

15. Arrange the glazed chicken thighs in a disposable aluminum pan and return it to the Big Green Egg.

16. Smoke the glazed chicken thighs for 30 minutes or until the internal temperature reaches 165°F (74°C), and remove them from the Big Green Egg.

17. Arrange the smoked chicken thighs on a serving dish and serve.

18. Enjoy!

PISTACHIO ALMOND RUB SMOKED WHOLE CHICKEN

(COOKING TIME 4 HOURS 10 MINUTES)

INGREDIENTS FOR 10 SERVINGS

- Whole chicken (4-lbs., 1.8-kg.)

THE INJECTION

- Unsalted butter - ¼ cup
- Apple juice - ¼ cup
- Brown sugar - 2 tablespoons
- Garlic powder - 1 teaspoon
- Ground black pepper - 1 teaspoon
- Salt - ½ teaspoon

THE RUB

- Ground pistachio - ½ cup
- Ground almond - ¼ cup
- Oregano - ½ cup
- Allspice - 2 tablespoons
- Salt - 1 teaspoon
- Black pepper - ½ teaspoon

THE GLAZE

- Unsalted butter - 3 tablespoons
- Honey - 2 tablespoons

THE HEAT

- Lump charcoal
- Mix of Maple and Oak wood chips

THE WATER BATH

- Water – 2 cups

- Ginger - 1 teaspoon

METHOD

1. Prepare the injection ingredients and melt the butter.

2. Once the butter is melted, add apple juice together with brown sugar, garlic powder, ground black pepper, and salt. Stir until incorporated.

3. Fill an injector with the spice mixture and inject it into the chicken. Set aside.

4. Next, combine the ground pistachio with almond then season it with oregano, allspice, salt, and black pepper. Mix well.

5. Apply the rub mixture over the chicken and set aside.

6. After that, fill the Big Green Egg with lump charcoal and starters then ignite the starters.

7. Sprinkle wood chips over the lump charcoal or place the wood chips in a stainless woodchip box.

8. Set a convEGGtor or a plate setter in the Big Green Egg and put a disposable aluminum pan on it.

9. Pour water into the aluminum pan and add ginger to it. Set the grill grate on top.

10. Close the Big Green Egg with the lid and set the vent to reach 275°F (135°C).

11. When the big is ready, place the seasoned chicken on the grill grate inside the Big Green Egg and smoke it for 4 hours.

12. Regularly check the internal temperature of the smoked chicken and once it reaches 170°F (77°C), take it out of the Big Green Egg.

13. Quickly combine butter with honey and glaze it over the smoked chicken.

14. Wrap the glazed smoked chicken with aluminum foil and let it rest for 30 minutes.

15. After 30 minutes, unwrap the smoked chicken and transfer it to a serving dish.

16. Cut the smoked chicken into slices and serve.

17. Enjoy!

Buttermilk Brine Smoked Chicken Wings with Pepper and Cayenne

(Cooking Time 2 Hours 10 Minutes)

Ingredients for 10 servings

- Chicken wings (5-lb., 2.3-kg.)

THE BRINE

- Buttermilk - 4 cups

- Salt - ½ cup

- Sugar - 3 tablespoons

- Black pepper - ½ teaspoon

THE RUB

- Cayenne pepper - ½ teaspoon

- Salt - 1 ¼ teaspoon

- Pepper - ¼ teaspoon

THE HEAT

- Lump charcoal

- Mix of Maple and Peach wood chips

THE WATER BATH

- Water – 2 cups

METHOD

1. Season the buttermilk with salt, sugar, and black pepper. Stir until incorporated.

2. Score the chicken wings at several places and add them to the brine mixture.

3. Soak the chicken wings overnight and store them in the fridge to keep the chicken wings fresh.

4. On the next day, remove the chicken wings from the fridge and thaw them at room temperature.

5. Take the chicken wings out of the brine and strain well.

6. Sprinkle cayenne pepper, salt, and pepper over the chicken wings and set aside.

7. Next, fill the Big Green Egg with lump charcoal and starters then ignite the starters.

8. Sprinkle wood chips over the lump charcoal or place the wood chips in a stainless woodchip box.

9. Set a convEGGtor or a plate setter in the Big Green Egg and put a disposable aluminum pan on it.

10. Pour water into the aluminum pan and set the grill grate on top.

11. Close the Big Green Egg with the lid and set the vent to reach 275°F (135°C).

12. Arrange the seasoned chicken wings on the grill grate inside the Big Green Egg and smoke them for 2 hours.

13. Once the internal temperature of the smoked chicken wings reaches 170°F (77°C), remove them from the Big Green Egg.

14. Arrange the smoked chicken wings on a serving dish and serve.

15. Enjoy!

Balsamic Smoked Chicken Breast with Spicy Tomato Glaze

(Cooking Time 3 Hours 10 Minutes)

Ingredients for 10 servings

- Boneless chicken breast (4-lbs., 1.8-kg.)

THE MARINADE

- Balsamic vinegar - ½ cup
- Olive oil - ½ cup
- Brown sugar - ¼ cup
- Salt - 1 teaspoon
- Pepper - ½ teaspoon
- Minced garlic - 1 tablespoon
- Fresh chopped basil - 2 tablespoons

THE GLAZE

- Tomato paste - ¼ cup
- Honey - 3 tablespoons
- Olive oil - 2 tablespoons
- Balsamic vinegar - 3 tablespoons
- Sesame oil - 1 teaspoon
- Black pepper - ¼ teaspoon
- Salt - A pinch
- Red chili flakes - 2 teaspoons
- Cayenne pepper - ½ teaspoon

The Heat

- Lump charcoal

- Mix of Oak and Pear wood chips

The Water Bath

- Water - 2 cups

Method

1. Mix the marinade ingredients--balsamic vinegar, olive oil, brown sugar, salt, pepper, minced garlic, and chopped basil in a container.

2. Score the chicken breast at several places and rub it with the seasoning mixture.

3. Marinate the chicken breast for at least 6 hours or overnight and store it in the fridge to keep the chicken breast fresh.

4. On the next day, take the chicken breast out of the fridge and thaw it at room temperature.

5. Next, fill the Big Green Egg with lump charcoal and starters then ignite the starters.

6. Sprinkle wood chips over the lump charcoal or place the wood chips in a stainless woodchip box.

7. Set a convEGGtor or a plate setter in the Big Green Egg and put a disposable aluminum pan on it.

8. Pour water into the aluminum pan and set the grill grate on top.

9. Close the Big Green Egg with the lid and set the vent to reach 275°F (135°C).

10. Place the marinated chicken breast on the grill inside the Big Green Egg and smoke it for 2 hours.

11. In the meantime, combine the glaze ingredients--tomato paste, honey, olive oil, balsamic vinegar, sesame oil, black pepper, salt, red chili flakes, and cayenne pepper. Stir until incorporated.

12. After 2 hours of smoking, baste the glaze mixture over the smoked chicken breast and wrap it with aluminum foil.

13. Return the wrapped chicken breast to the Big Green Egg and continue smoking for another hour.

14. Once the internal temperature of the smoked chicken breast reaches 170°F (77°C), remove it from the Big Green Egg.

15. Let the wrapped smoked chicken breast rest for approximately 30 minutes and unwrap it.

16. Sprinkle chopped basil on top and serve.

17. Enjoy!

TURKEY

ORANGE MARMALADE SMOKED CHICKEN WITH FRESH HERBS AND CELERIES

(COOKING TIME 3 HOURS 30 MINUTES)

INGREDIENTS FOR 10 SERVINGS

- Whole turkey (14-lbs., 6.3-kg.)

THE RUB

- Fresh chopped celery - ¼ cup
- Fresh chopped rosemary - 2 tablespoons
- Fresh chopped thyme - 1 tablespoon
- Fresh chopped sage - ½ tablespoon
- Fresh oranges - 2
- Garlic cloves - 6

THE GLAZE

- Orange marmalade - ¾ cup
- Orange juice - ¾ cup
- Avocado oil - 3 tablespoons
- Soy sauce - 1 ½ tablespoon
- Minced rosemary - 2 tablespoons
- Black pepper - 1 tablespoon

THE HEAT

- Lump charcoal
- Mix of Alder and Apple wood chips

THE WATER BATH

- Chicken broth - 2 cups
- White wine - ¼ cup

METHOD

1. Cut the fresh oranges into slices then mix them with celery, rosemary, thyme, sage, and garlic cloves.

2. Take half of the seasoning mixture and fill it into the turkey cavity.

3. Apply the remaining seasoning mixture over the turkey and set aside.

4. Next, fill the Big Green Egg with lump charcoal and starters then ignite the starters.

5. Sprinkle wood chips over the lump charcoal or place the wood chips in a stainless woodchip box.

6. Set a convEGGtor or a plate setter in the Big Green Egg and put a disposable aluminum pan on it.

7. Pour chicken broth and white wine into the aluminum pan and set a grill grate on top.

8. Close the Big Green Egg with the lid and set the vent to reach 325°F (163°C).

9. When the Big Green Egg is ready, place the seasoned turkey on the grill grate inside the Big Green Egg and smoke it for 2 hours.

10. In the meantime, combine the orange marmalade with orange juice, avocado oil, and soy sauce.

11. Add black pepper to the glaze mixture and stir well.

12. After 2 hours of smoking, remove the smoked turkey from the Big Green Egg and glaze it with the orange marmalade mixture.

13. Wrap the turkey with aluminum foil and return it back to the Big Green Egg.

14. Continue smoking for an hour and a half and check the internal temperature.

15. Once it reaches 165°F (74°C), take the smoked turkey out of the Big Green Egg.

16. Unwrap the smoked turkey and serve.

17. Enjoy!

Beer Brine Smoked Turkey Wings with Spicy Seasoning

(Cooking Time 2 Hours 10 Minutes)

Ingredients for 10 servings

- Turkey wings (5-lb., 2.3-kg.)

The Brine

- Cold water -2 cups

- Beer - 1 bottle large beer

- White vinegar - 2 tablespoons

- White sugar - 2 tablespoons

- Salt - 2 tablespoons

THE RUB

- Chipotle chili powder - 1 tablespoon

- Brown sugar - 1 tablespoon

- Paprika - ½ tablespoon

- Garlic powder - 1 tablespoon

- Oregano - 1 teaspoon

- Dried parsley - ½ teaspoon

- Dried thyme - ½ teaspoon

- Cayenne pepper - ½ teaspoon

- Salt - ¼ teaspoon

- Olive oil - 2 tablespoons

- Hot sauce - 3 tablespoons

- Honey - 1 tablespoon

THE HEAT

- Lump charcoal

- Cherry wood chips

THE WATER BATH

- Water - 2 cups

METHOD

1. Pour water, beer, and white vinegar into a container. Stir well.

2. Season the mixture with sugar and salt then mix until dissolved.

3. Add the turkey wings to the brine mixture and soak them overnight.

4. Store them in the fridge to keep the turkey wings fresh.

5. On the next day, take the turkey wings out of the brine then wash and rinse them. Pat them dry.

6. Next, combine chipotle chili powder, paprika, brown sugar, garlic powder, oregano, parsley, thyme, cayenne, pepper, and salt in a container.

7. Drizzle olive oil, hot sauce, and honey over the seasoning and stir until becoming a paste.

8. Apply the seasoning paste over the turkey wings and set aside.

9. Fill the Big Green Egg with lump charcoal and starters then ignite the starters.

10. Sprinkle wood chips over the lump charcoal or place the wood chips in a stainless woodchip box.

11. Set a convEGGtor or a plate setter in the Big Green Egg and put a disposable aluminum pan on it.

12. Pour water into the aluminum pan and set a grill grate on top.

13. Close the Big Green Egg with the lid and set the vent to reach 250°F (121°C).

14. Arrange the seasoned turkey wings on the grill grate inside the Big Green Egg and smoke them for 2 hours.

15. Regularly check the internal temperature of the smoked turkey wings and once it reaches 160°F (71°C), remove them from the Big Green Egg. Serve and enjoy.

CRANBERRY GINGER SMOKED TURKEY BREAST

(COOKING TIME 2 HOURS 10 MINUTES)

INGREDIENTS FOR 10 SERVINGS

- Boneless turkey breast (5-lb., 2.3-kg.)

THE BRINE

- Cold water - 3 cups

- White wine - 1 cup

- Orange juice - 1 ½ cup

- Salt - ½ cup

- Brown sugar - 1.2 cup

- Ground ginger - 2 tablespoons

- Bay leaves - 2

- Fresh thyme - 2 sprigs

THE SAUCE

- Chopped fresh cranberries - 2 cups

- Grated ginger - ½ teaspoon

- Grated orange zest - 1 teaspoon

- White sugar - ½ cup

- Orange juice - ½ cup

- Water - 3 tablespoons

THE HEAT

- Lump charcoal

- Cherry wood chips

THE WATER BATH

- Orange juice - 2 cups

METHOD

1. Pour cold water into a container then mix it with white wine and orange juice.

2. Season the liquid mixture with salt, brown sugar, ground ginger, bay leaves, and thyme. Mix until dissolved.

3. Score the turkey breast at several places and put it into the brine mixture.

4. Soak the turkey breast for at least 8 hours or overnight and store it in the fridge to keep the turkey breast fresh.

5. On the next day, remove the turkey breast from the fridge and thaw it at room temperature.

6. Take the turkey breast out of the brine then wash and rinse it. Pat it dry.

7. Next, fill the Big Green Egg with lump charcoal and starters then ignite the starters.

8. Sprinkle wood chips over the lump charcoal or place the wood chips in a stainless woodchip box.

9. Set a convEGGtor or a plate setter in the Big Green Egg and put a disposable aluminum pan on it.

10. Pour orange juice into the aluminum pan and set a grill grate on top.

11. Close the Big Green Egg with the lid and set the vent to reach 250°F (121°C).

12. Place the seasoned turkey breast on the grill grate inside the Big Green Egg and smoke it for 2 hours.

13. In the meantime, place chopped cranberries, grated ginger, grated orange zest, sugar, orange juice, and water in a saucepan.

14. Stir well and bring the sauce to a simmer.

15. Remove the sauce from heat and strain well. Set aside.

16. Once the internal temperature of the smoked turkey breast reaches 160°F (71°C), remove it from the Big Green Egg.

17. Cut the smoked turkey breast into thin slices and drizzle the sauce over it.

18. Serve and enjoy!

CRISPY SKIN SMOKED TURKEY BREAST WITH BROWN SUGAR GARLIC MARINADE

(COOKING TIME 2 HOURS 10 MINUTES)

INGREDIENTS FOR 10 SERVINGS

- Boneless turkey breast (5-lb., 2.3-kg.)

THE MARINADE

- Minced garlic - ¼ cup

- Brown sugar - ¼ cup

- Olive oil - 3 tablespoons

- Worcestershire sauce - 3 tablespoons

- Soy sauce - ¼ cup

- Dijon mustard - 2 tablespoons

- Salt - 1 ¼ teaspoon

THE GLAZE

- Butter - 3 tablespoons

- Honey - 3 tablespoons

THE HEAT

- Lump charcoal

- Mix of Cherry and Pecan wood chips

THE WATER BATH

- Water - 2 cups

METHOD

1. Rub the turkey breast with minced garlic, brown sugar, olive oil, Worcestershire sauce, soy sauce, Dijon mustard, and salt.

2. Marinate the turkey for at least 4 hours and store it in the fridge to keep them fresh.

3. After 4 hours, take the turkey breast out of the fridge and thaw it at room temperature. Set aside.

4. Next, fill the Big Green Egg with lump charcoal and starters then ignite the starters.

5. Sprinkle wood chips over the lump charcoal or place the wood chips in a stainless woodchip box.

6. Set a convEGGtor or a plate setter in the Big Green Egg and put a disposable aluminum pan on it.

7. Pour water into the aluminum pan and set a grill grate on top.

8. Close the Big Green Egg with the lid and set the vent to reach 250°F (121°C).

9. Place the seasoned turkey breast on the grill grate inside the Big Green Egg and smoke it for an hour and a half. The internal temperature of the smoked turkey breast will be around 145°F (63°C).

10. In the meantime, combine butter with honey and stir well.

11. After an hour of smoking, increase the temperature of the Big Green Egg to 350°F (177°C) and baste the glaze mixture over the smoked turkey breast.

12. Continue smoking for 30 minutes or until the internal temperature of the smoked turkey breast reaches 165°F (74°C).

13. Remove the smoked turkey breast from Big Green Egg and transfer it to a serving dish. Serve and enjoy.

CHAPTER-6 FISH

MAPLE GLAZED SWEET SMOKED SALMON

(COOKING TIME 30 MINUTES)

INGREDIENTS FOR 10 SERVINGS

- Salmon fillet (3,5-lb., 2.3-kg.)

THE BRINE

- Brown sugar - 2 cups
- Salt - ¼ cup
- Honey - ¾ cup
- Maples syrup - 2 tablespoons
- Cold water - 1 quart

THE GLAZE

- Maple syrup - 3 tablespoons

THE HEAT

- Lump charcoal

- Mix of Alder and Mulberry wood chips

METHOD

1. Add brown sugar, salt, honey, and maple syrup to the water. Stir until dissolved.

2. Put the salmon fillet into the brine mixture and soak it for approximately 4 hours. Store it in the fridge or add some ice cubes to the brine to keep the salmon fillet fresh.

3. After 4 hours, take the salmon fillet out of the brine and strain well.

4. Next, fill the Big Green Egg with lump charcoal and starters then ignite the starters.

5. Sprinkle wood chips over the lump charcoal or place the wood chips in a stainless woodchip box.

6. Set a convEGGtor or a plate setter in the Big Green Egg and set a grill grate on top.

7. Close the Big Green Egg with the lid and set the vent to reach 200°F (93°C).

8. Wait until the Big Green Egg is ready and place the salmon fillet on the grill grate.

9. Smoke the salmon for 30 minutes and baste maple syrup over it once every 15 minutes.

10. Once it is done, remove the smoked salmon from the Big Green Egg and arrange it on a serving dish. Serve and enjoy.

WHITE WINE SMOKED HALIBUT WITH TARRAGON

(COOKING TIME 30 MINUTES)

INGREDIENTS FOR 10 SERVINGS

- Halibut fillet (3-lb., 1.4-kg.)

THE MARINADE

- Dry white wine - ¾ cup
- Olive oil - ¼ cup
- Lemon juice - 3 tablespoons
- Minced garlic - 2 tablespoons
- Salt - ½ teaspoon
- Black pepper - ½ teaspoon

THE RUB

- Brown sugar - 3 tablespoons

THE HEAT

- Lump charcoal

- Mix of Alder and Mulberry wood chips

METHOD

1. Combine dry white wine with olive oil, lemon juice, minced garlic, salt, and black pepper.

2. Rub the seasoning mixture over the halibut fillet and marinate for 4 hours. Store it in the fridge to keep the halibut fresh.

3. After 4 hours, take the marinated halibut out of the fridge and thaw it at room temperature. Sprinkle brown sugar on top.

4. Next, fill the Big Green Egg with lump charcoal and starters then ignite the starters.

5. Sprinkle wood chips over the lump charcoal or place the wood chips in a stainless woodchip box.

6. Set a convEGGtor or a plate setter in the Big Green Egg and set a grill grate on top.

7. Close the Big Green Egg with the lid and set the vent to reach 200°F (93°C).

8. Wait until the Big Green Egg is ready and arrange the seasoned halibut fillet on the grill grate.

9. Smoke the halibut fillet for 30 minutes or until it flakes.

10. Remove the smoked halibut from the Big Green Egg and serve.

11. Enjoy!

Savory Smoked Red Snapper with Lemon and Herbs

(Cooking Time 45 Minutes)

Ingredients for 10 servings

- Whole red snapper (4-lbs., 1.8-kg.)

The Marinade

- Lemon juice - ¼ cup
- Olive oil - 3 tablespoons
- Chopped fresh basil - 1 tablespoon
- Chopped fresh thyme
- Salt - 1 teaspoon
- Pepper - ½ teaspoon

113

The Rub

- Grated lemon zest - 1 teaspoon
- Dried basil - 2 teaspoons
- Oregano - 2 teaspoons
- Dried thyme - 1 ½ teaspoon
- Salt - ¼ teaspoon

The Heat

- Lump charcoal
- Mesquite wood chips

Method

1. Pour lemon juice and olive oil into a container.
2. Season the liquid mixture with fresh basil, thyme, salt, and pepper.
3. Add the red snappers to the seasoning mixture and marinate for at least 2 hours.
4. In the meantime, combine grated lemon zest, basil, oregano, thyme, and salt. Mix well.
5. After 2 hours, take the red snappers from the marinade and rub them with the grated lemon zest mixture. Set aside.
6. Next, fill the Big Green Egg with lump charcoal and starters then ignite the starters.
7. Sprinkle wood chips over the lump charcoal or place the wood chips in a stainless woodchip box.

8. Set a convEGGtor or a plate setter in the Big Green Egg and set a grill grate on top.

9. Close the Big Green Egg with the lid and set the vent to reach 200°F (93°C).

10. Once the Big Green Egg reaches the desired temperature, arrange the seasoned red snappers on the grill grate inside it and smoke for 45 minutes.

11. Check the internal temperature of the smoked red snappers and once it reaches 145°F (63°C), remove the smoked red snappers from the Big Green Egg.

12. Serve and enjoy!

Aromatic Refreshing Smoked Tilapia with Tangerine Marinade

(Cooking Time 30 Minutes)

Ingredients for 10 servings

- Tilapia fillet (4-lbs., 1.8-kg.)

THE MARINADE

- Tangerine juice - 2 cups

- Lemon juice - ¼ cup

- Olive oil - 2 tablespoons

- Soy sauce - 2 tablespoons

- Brown sugar - 3 tablespoons

- Salt - 1 teaspoon

- Cumin - 1 teaspoon

- Black pepper - ½ teaspoon

- Red pepper - ½ teaspoon

- Garlic powder - 1 tablespoon

- Paprika - 1 teaspoon

THE HEAT

- Lump charcoal

- Mix of Cherry and Apple wood chips

METHOD

1. Combine tangerine juice with lemon juice, olive oil, and soy sauce.

2. Add brown sugar, salt, cumin, black pepper, red pepper, garlic powder, and paprika to the liquid mixture. Stir until dissolved.

3. Put the tilapia fillet into the liquid mixture and marinate it for at least 4 hours. Store the tilapia fillet in the fridge to keep it fresh.

4. After 4 hours, take the marinated tilapia fillet out of the fridge and thaw it at room temperature.

5. Next, fill the Big Green Egg with lump charcoal and starters then ignite the starters.

6. Sprinkle wood chips over the lump charcoal or place the wood chips in a stainless woodchip box.

7. Set a convEGGtor or a plate setter in the Big Green Egg and set a grill grate on top.

8. Close the Big Green Egg with the lid and set the vent to reach 200°F (93°C).

9. Arrange the marinated tilapia on the grill grate inside the Big Green Egg and smoke it for 30 minutes or until it flakes.

10. Once it is done, remove the smoked tilapia from the Big Green Egg and transfer it to a serving dish.

11. Serve and enjoy.

Chapter-7 SEAFOOD

Smoked Squid with Spicy and Sweet Soy Sauce

(Cooking Time 1 Hour)

Ingredients for 10 servings

- Fresh squids (3-lb., 1.4-kg.)

THE MARINADE

- Minced garlic - 2 tablespoons

- Coriander - 1 tablespoon

THE GLAZE

- Olive oil - 3 tablespoons

THE SAUCE

- Minced garlic - 1 teaspoon

- Minced shallot - 1 teaspoon

- Chili powder - 1 teaspoon

- Kaffir lime leaves - 1

THE HEAT

- Lump charcoal

- Cherry wood chips

METHOD

1. Wash the fresh squids but keep the ink stays.

2. Rub the fresh squids with the coriander and minced garlic and let them rest for a few minutes.

3. Next, fill the Big Green Egg with lump charcoal and starters then ignite the starters.

4. Sprinkle wood chips over the lump charcoal or place the wood chips in a stainless woodchip box.

5. Set a convEGGtor or a plate setter in the Big Green Egg and set a grill grate on top.

6. Close the Big Green Egg with the lid and set the vent to reach 275°F (135°C).

7. Arrange the squids on the grill grate in the Big Green Egg and smoke them for an hour. Baste olive oil over the squids several times.

8. In the meantime, season the soy sauce with garlic, shallot, and chili. Stir well.

9. Once the smoked squids flake, remove from the Big Green Egg and transfer to a serving dish.

10. Baste the sauce over the smoked squids and serve.

11. Enjoy!

Cheesy Butter Smoked Lobster

(Cooking Time 45 Minutes)

Ingredients for 10 servings

- Fresh lobsters (4-lbs., 1.8-kg.)

The Seasoning

- Lemon juice - ½ cup

- Garlic powder - 2 teaspoons

- Diced onion - 2 tablespoons

- Salted butter - 3 tablespoons

- Diced parsley - 2 teaspoons

- Black pepper - ½ teaspoon

- Grated parmesan cheese - 3 tablespoons

THE HEAT

- Lump charcoal
- Mix of Alder and Cherry wood chips

METHOD

1. Combine lemon juice, garlic powder, diced onion, salted butter, parsley, black pepper, and grated Parmesan cheese. Mix well.

2. Using sharp scissors cut the lobster's shell and top each lobster with the cheesy butter mixture.

3. Next, fill the Big Green Egg with lump charcoal and starters then ignite the starters.

4. Sprinkle wood chips over the lump charcoal or place the wood chips in a stainless woodchip box.

5. Set a convEGGtor or a plate setter in the Big Green Egg and set a grill grate on top.

6. Close the Big Green Egg with the lid and set the vent to reach 275°F (135°C).

7. Arrange the lobsters on the grill grate inside the Big Green Egg and smoke for 45 minutes.

8. Once it is done, remove the smoked lobsters from the Big Green Egg and transfer them to a serving dish.

9. Serve and enjoy.

OLD BAY SEASONING SMOKED CRAB

(COOKING TIME 1 HOUR)

INGREDIENTS FOR 10 SERVINGS

- Crabs (6-lb., 2.7-kg.)

THE RUB

- Salt - 1 ½ teaspoon

- Celery seed - 1 ½ teaspoon

- Sweet paprika - 1 tablespoon

- Smoked paprika - 1 teaspoon

- Dry mustard - 1 ½ teaspoon

- Grated ginger - 1 teaspoon

- Black pepper - 1 teaspoon

- White pepper - ½ teaspoon

- Red chili flakes - ½ teaspoon

- Ground nutmeg - ¼ teaspoon

- Ground cinnamon - ¼ teaspoon

- Ground cloves - A pinch

- Ground cardamom - ¼ teaspoon

- Ground allspice - ¼ teaspoon

THE HEAT

- Lump charcoal

- Mix of Alder and Cherry wood chips

METHOD

1. Combine the entire seasoning ingredients--salt, celery seeds, sweet paprika, smoked paprika, mustard, ginger, black pepper, white pepper, red chili flakes, nutmeg, cinnamon, cloves, cardamom, and allspice. Mix well.

2. Place the crabs on a sheet of aluminum foil and sprinkle the seasoning mixture over them.

3. Wrap the crabs with aluminum foil and set them aside.

4. Next, fill the Big Green Egg with lump charcoal and starters then ignite the starters.

5. Sprinkle wood chips over the lump charcoal or place the wood chips in a stainless woodchip box.

6. Set a convEGGtor or a plate setter in the Big Green Egg and set a grill grate on top.

7. Close the Big Green Egg with the lid and set the vent to reach 250°F (121°C).

8. Insert the wrapped carbs into the Big Green Egg and smoke for an hour.

9. Once the smoked crabs are done, remove them from the Big Green Egg and unwrap them.

10. Transfer the smoked crabs to a serving dish and serve.

11. Enjoy!

GINGER BRINE SMOKED SCALLOPS

(COOKING TIME 30 MINUTES)

INGREDIENTS FOR 10 SERVINGS

- Scallops (4-lbs., 1.8-kg.)

THE BRINE

- Ground ginger - 1 tablespoon

- Brown sugar - ¾ cup

- Soy sauce - ¾ cup

- Oyster sauce - 2 tablespoons

- Garlic powder - 1 tablespoon

- Cold water - 1 quart

THE HEAT

- Lump charcoal

- Cherry wood chips

METHOD

1. Add ginger, brown sugar, soy sauce, oyster sauce, and garlic powder to the cold water. Stir until dissolved.

2. Put the scallops into the brine mixture and soak for an hour.

3. After an hour, strain the scallops and pat them dry.

4. Next, fill the Big Green Egg with lump charcoal and starters then ignite the starters.

5. Sprinkle wood chips over the lump charcoal or place the wood chips in a stainless woodchip box.

6. Set a convEGGtor or a plate setter in the Big Green Egg and set a grill grate on top.

7. Close the Big Green Egg with the lid and set the vent to reach 200°F (93°C).

8. Spread the scallops in a disposable aluminum pan and insert them into the Big Green Egg.

9. Smoke the scallops for 30 minutes or until the smoked scallops are translucent.

10. Take the smoked scallops out of the Big Green Egg and transfer them to a serving dish.

11. Serve and enjoy.

CHAPTER-8 GAME

SALTED BUTTER SMOKED PIGEON BREAST WITH BOURBON GLAZE

(COOKING TIME 2 HOURS 30 MINUTES)

INGREDIENTS FOR 10 SERVINGS

- Boneless pigeon breast (4-lbs., 1.8-kg.)

THE BRINE

- Salt - 1 ½ teaspoon

- Sugar - 1 tablespoon

THE RUB

- Salted butter - ½ cup

- Garlic powder - 2 teaspoons

- Onion powder - 1 teaspoon

- Dried sage - 1 teaspoon

- Dried thyme - 1 teaspoon

- Black pepper - 1 teaspoon

- Brown sugar - 3 tablespoons

THE GLAZE

- Bourbon - ½ cup

- Brown sugar - ½ cup

- Salt - A pinch

THE HEAT

- Lump charcoal

- Apple wood chips

THE WATER BATH

- Water - 2 cups

- Fresh lemon - 1

METHOD

1. Rub salt and sugar over the pigeon breast and cover it with plastic wrap. Refrigerate the pigeon breast for at least 4 hours.

2. Next, take the pigeon breast out of the refrigerator and unwrap them.

3. Baste salted butter over the pigeon breast and rub it with a mixture of garlic powder, onion powder, dried sage, thyme, black pepper, and brown sugar. Set aside.

4. Fill the Big Green Egg with lump charcoal and starters then ignite the starters.

5. Sprinkle wood chips over the lump charcoal or place the wood chips in a stainless woodchip box.

6. Set a convEGGtor or a plate setter in the Big Green Egg and put a disposable aluminum pan on it.

7. Pour water into the aluminum pan and add sliced lemon to it. Set a grill grate on top.

8. Close the Big Green Egg with the lid and set the vent to reach 250°F (121°C).

9. Wait until the Big Green Egg reaches the desired temperature and arrange the seasoned pigeon breast on the grill grate inside it.

10. Smoke the pigeon breast for 2 hours or until the internal temperature of the pigeon breast reaches 160°F (71°C).

11. In the meantime, combine bourbon, brown sugar, and salt in a disposable aluminum pan. Set aside.

12. After 2 hours of smoking remove the pigeon breast from the Big Green Egg and place them in the disposable aluminum pan with the glaze mixture.

13. Roll the pigeon breast and make sure that it is completely coated with the glaze mixture.

14. Return the glazed pigeon breast to the Big Green Egg and continue smoking until the internal temperature reaches 165°F (74°C).

15. Once it is done, remove the smoked pigeon breast from the Big Green Egg and transfer it to a serving dish.

16. Cut the smoked pigeon breast into thick slices and serve.

17. Enjoy!

(COOKING TIME 3 HOURS 10 MINUTES)

INGREDIENTS FOR 10 SERVINGS

- Whole doves (5-lb., 2.3-kg.)

THE MARINADE

- Brown sugar - ¾ cup
- Olive oil - 3 tablespoons
- Ground cinnamon - 2 tablespoons
- Salt - ½ teaspoons
- Paprika - 2 teaspoons
- Ground black pepper - 1 teaspoon

THE RUB

- Ground coffee - ¼ cup
- Cocoa powder - ¼ cup
- Ground cinnamon - 1 ½ teaspoon
- Brown sugar - ¼ cup
- Chili powder - 2 teaspoons
- Ground anise seed - 2 teaspoons
- Salt - 1 teaspoon

THE HEAT

- Lump charcoal
- Mix of Pecan and Apple wood chips

THE WATER BATH

- Brewed coffee – 2 cups

METHOD

1. Mix brown sugar with ground cinnamon, salt, paprika, and black pepper in a bowl.

2. Drizzle olive oil over the spice mixture and stir until becoming a paste.

3. Rub the mixture over the doves and marinate them for at least 4 hours. Store the marinated doves in the fridge to keep them fresh.

4. In the meantime, combine the rub ingredients--ground coffee, cocoa powder, cinnamon, brown sugar, chili powder, ground anise seed, and salt. Mix well.

5. Use your hand to apply the rub ingredients over each dove. Set aside.

6. Next, fill the Big Green Egg with lump charcoal and starters then ignite the starters.

7. Sprinkle wood chips over the lump charcoal or place the wood chips in a stainless woodchip box.

8. Set a convEGGtor or a plate setter in the Big Green Egg and put a disposable aluminum pan on it.

9. Pour brewed coffee into the aluminum pan and set the grill grate on top.

10. Close the Big Green Egg with the lid and set the vent to reach 275°F (135°C).

11. Arrange the seasoned doves on the grill grate inside the Big Green Egg and smoked them for 3 hours.

12. Once the internal temperature of the smoked doves reaches 170°F (77°C), remove the doves from the Big Green Egg and transfer them to a serving dish.

13. Serve and enjoy.

THYME AND RED ONION STUFFED SMOKED GOOSE

(COOKING TIME 3 HOURS 10 MINUTES)

INGREDIENTS FOR **10** SERVINGS

- Whole goose (4-lbs., 1.8-kg.)

The Marinade

- Olive oil - 3 tablespoons

- Lemon juice - 3 tablespoons

- Minced garlic - 1 tablespoon

- Ground mustard - ½ teaspoon

- Diced fresh dill - 1 teaspoon

- Maple syrup - 2 tablespoons

- Brown sugar - 3 tablespoons

The Filling

- Chopped red onion - 1 cup

- Fresh thyme - 5 sprigs

- Garlic - 5 cloves

- Fresh lemons - 2

The Heat

- Lump charcoal

- Hickory wood chips

The Water Bath

- Water - 2 cups

- Lemon juice - 2 tablespoons

METHOD

1. Combine the marinade ingredients--olive oil, lemon juice, minced garlic, ground mustard, fresh dill, maple syrup, and brown sugar. Mix well.

2. Apply the spice mixture over the goose and set it aside.

3. Next, cut the fresh lemon into slices and mix them with chopped red onion, thyme, and garlic cloves.

4. Fill the goose cavity with the lemon mixture and set aside.

5. Next, fill the Big Green Egg with lump charcoal and starters then ignite the starters.

6. Sprinkle wood chips over the lump charcoal or place the wood chips in a stainless woodchip box.

7. Set a convEGGtor or a plate setter in the Big Green Egg and put a disposable aluminum pan on it.

8. Pour water and lemon juice into the aluminum pan and set the grill grate on top.

9. Close the Big Green Egg with the lid and set the vent to reach 275°F (135°C).

10. Once the Big Green Egg is ready, insert the stuffed goose into it and smoke for 3 hours.

11. Regularly check the internal temperature of the smoked goose and once it reaches 165°F (74°C), remove it from the Big Green Egg.

12. Transfer the smoked goose to a serving dish and serve.

13. Enjoy!

Sweet Butter Smoked Venison Ribs with Chili

(Cooking Time 4 Hours 10 Minutes)

Ingredients for 10 servings

- Venison ribs (7-lb., 3.2-kg.)

THE RUB

- Garlic powder - 1 ½ tablespoon
- Pepper - 1 teaspoon
- Paprika - 2 teaspoons
- Salt - 2 teaspoons
- Mustard powder - 1 tablespoon
- Chili powder - 1 ½ teaspoons
- Cumin - 1 teaspoon
- Dried thyme - 1 tablespoon
- Brown sugar - 3 tablespoons

THE SPRAY

- Apple juice - 1 cup

THE GLAZE

- Butter - 3 tablespoons
- Soy sauce - 3 tablespoons
- Brown sugar - 3 tablespoons

THE HEAT

- Lump charcoal
- Mix of Pecan, Apple, and Hickory wood chips

THE WATER BATH

- Water - 2 cups

METHOD

1. Mix garlic powder, with paprika, pepper, salt, mustard, chili powder, cumin, dried thyme, and brown sugar. Stir until combined.

2. Score the venison ribs at several places and rub the spice mixture over the ribs. Set aside.

3. Next, fill the Big Green Egg with lump charcoal and starters then ignite the starters.

4. Sprinkle wood chips over the lump charcoal or place the wood chips in a stainless woodchip box.

5. Set a convEGGtor or a plate setter in the Big Green Egg and put a disposable aluminum pan on it.

6. Pour water into the aluminum pan and set the grill grate on top.

7. Close the Big Green Egg with the lid and set the vent to reach 275°F (135°C).

8. Place the seasoned venison ribs on the grill grate inside the Big Green Egg and smoke for 4 hours.

9. Spray apple juice over the venison ribs once every 30 minutes and smoke the ribs until the internal temperature reaches 165°F (74°C).

10. In the meantime, melt butter and combine it with soy sauce and brown sugar. Stir until incorporated.

11. Once the smoked venison ribs are done, remove them from the Big Green Egg and place the ribs on a sheet of aluminum foil.

12. Baste the butter mixture over the ribs and wrap it with aluminum foil.

13. Let the ribs rest for approximately 30 minutes and unwrap them.

14. Serve and enjoy.

CHAPTER-9 VEGETABLES

CHEESE AND NUTS STUFFED SMOKED RED PEPPER

(COOKING TIME 2 HOURS 10 MINUTES)

INGREDIENTS FOR 10 SERVINGS

- Sweet Red Peppers (2-lbs., 0.9-kg.)

THE FILLING

- Groundnuts - 1 cup

- Grated Parmesan cheese - 1 cup

- Diced parsley - 1 tablespoon

- Black pepper - ¼ teaspoon

- Ground nutmeg - A pinch

THE HEAT

- Lump charcoal
- Cherry wood chips

METHOD

1. Cut the top part of the peppers and remove the seeds. Set aside.

2. Combine groundnut with grated Parmesan cheese and season the mixture with parsley, black pepper, and nutmeg.

3. Fill each pepper with the cheese mixture and arrange them in a disposable aluminum pan.

4. Next, fill the Big Green Egg with lump charcoal and starters then ignite the starters.

5. Sprinkle wood chips over the lump charcoal or place the wood chips in a stainless woodchip box.

6. Set a convEGGtor or a plate setter in the Big Green Egg and put a disposable aluminum pan on it. Set a grill grate on top.

7. Close the Big Green Egg with the lid and set the vent to reach 225°F (107°C).

8. Insert the aluminum pan with stuffed peppers into the Big Green Egg and smoke the peppers for 2 hours.

9. Once it is done, remove the smoked peppers from the Big Green Egg and arrange them on a serving dish.

10. Serve and enjoy.

ROSEMARY SMOKED BRUSSELS SPROUTS WITH GARLIC AROMA

(COOKING TIME 1 HOUR 10 MINUTES)

INGREDIENTS FOR 10 SERVINGS

- Brussels Sprouts (2-lbs., 0.9-kg.)

THE RUB

- Diced fresh rosemary - 1 ½ teaspoon

- Minced garlic - 2 tablespoons

- Pepper - ½ teaspoon

- Salt - A pinch

- Onion powder - ½ teaspoon

- Olive oil - 1 tablespoon

THE HEAT

- Lump charcoal

- Cherry wood chips

Method

1. Fill the Big Green Egg with lump charcoal and starters then ignite the starters.

2. Sprinkle wood chips over the lump charcoal or place the wood chips in a stainless woodchip box.

3. Set a convEGGtor or a plate setter in the Big Green Egg and put a disposable aluminum pan on it. Set a grill grate on top.

4. Close the Big Green Egg with the lid and set the vent to reach 400°F (204°C).

5. Cut the Brussels sprouts into halves and rub them with rosemary, minced garlic, salt, pepper, onion powder, and olive oil.

6. Spread the seasoned Brussels sprouts in a disposable aluminum pan and insert it into the Big Green Egg.

7. Smoke the Brussels sprouts an hour and remove them from the Big Green Egg. Add more smoking time if you like the Brussels sprout to be tenderer.

8. Serve and enjoy!

Smoked Butternut Squash Puree with Maple Syrup

(Cooking Time 2 Hours 30 Minutes)

Ingredients for 10 servings

- Butternut squash (4-lbs., 1.8-kg.)

The Spices

- Butter - 3 tablespoons
- Salt - 1 teaspoon
- Black pepper - 1 teaspoon
- Onion powder - 2 teaspoons
- Maple Syrup - 3 tablespoons
- Ground cinnamon - ½ teaspoon
- Ground cloves - A pinch

THE HEAT

- Lump charcoal
- Cherry wood chips

METHOD

1. Fill the Big Green Egg with lump charcoal and starters then ignite the starters.

2. Sprinkle wood chips over the lump charcoal or place the wood chips in a stainless woodchip box.

3. Set a convEGGtor or a plate setter in the Big Green Egg and put a disposable aluminum pan on it. Set a grill grate on top.

4. Close the Big Green Egg with the lid and set the vent to reach 350°F (177°C).

5. Cut the butternut squash into halves lengthwise and baste butter over it.

6. Sprinkle salt, pepper, and onion powder on top then arrange the butternut squash on the grill grate inside the Big Green Egg.

7. Smoke the butternut squash approximately an hour on a half or until it is tender.

8. Once it is done, remove the smoked butternut squash from the Big Green Egg.

9. Quickly scoop out the smoked butternut squash and place the flesh in a bowl.

10. Add maple syrup, cinnamon, and cloves to the butternut squash then mash until smooth.

11. Serve and enjoy.

CINNAMON HONEY SMOKED TOMATOES

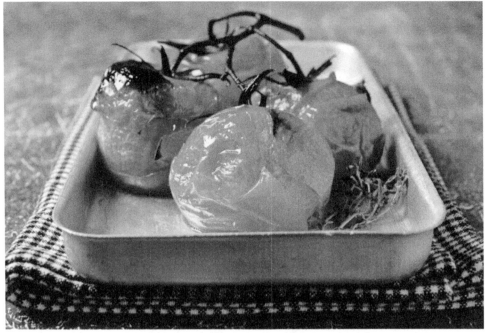

(COOKING TIME 40 MINUTES)

INGREDIENTS FOR 10 SERVINGS

- Red tomatoes (2-lbs., 0.9-kg.)

THE SPICES

- Honey - 2 tablespoons

- Brown sugar - 1 ½ tablespoon

- Salt - ¼ teaspoon

- Cinnamon - ¼ teaspoon

- Garlic powder - ¼ teaspoon

THE HEAT

- Lump charcoal

- Cherry wood chips

METHOD

1. Fill the Big Green Egg with lump charcoal and starters then ignite the starters.

2. Sprinkle wood chips over the lump charcoal or place the wood chips in a stainless woodchip box.

3. Set a convEGGtor or a plate setter in the Big Green Egg and put a disposable aluminum pan on it. Set a grill grate on top.

4. Close the Big Green Egg with the lid and set the vent to reach 200°F (93°C).

5. Arrange the whole red tomatoes in a disposable aluminum pan and drizzle honey over them.

6. Sprinkle garlic powder, salt, cinnamon, and brown sugar on top then insert the aluminum pan into the Big Green Egg.

7. Smoke the tomatoes for approximately 40 minutes or until tender then remove them from the Big Green Egg.

8. Transfer the smoked tomatoes to a serving dish and serve.

9. Enjoy!

CHAPTER-10 CERAMIC SMOKER

BIG GREEN EGG

To put it simply, Big Green EGG is essentially the name of one of the most well known as prolific manufacturer of famous Kamado Styled Ceramic BBQ Charcoal Cookers. But here's there thing, there are certain features that makes their appliance exceptional from other similar appliances in the market! Big GREEN EGG maintains the highest level of quality possible when choosing materials to build their grills, the EGGs themselves are extremely versatile and easy to use! Just a single EGG can be used for direct, indirect grilling as well as smoking and baking!

DIFFERENT SIZES OF BIG GREEN EGG

You should be aware that there are a number of different sizes that are available for you to purchase. The following section should give you a small breakdown of the different sizes that are available to you.

1) **Mini:** This model is the absolutely perfect for those individuals who want to carry it to a picnic or have a small home. This unit weighs about 36 pounds and has a grid diameter of 10 inches. It has the capacity to hold about 2 chicken breasts in one go.

2) **MiniMax:** This particular model is also awesome for camping and small parties. It is easy to carry and comes with a nifty and sturdy grip. It weighs 90 pounds and has a diameter of 13 inches. It can hold a 12 pounds turkey in one go.

3) **Small:** This is perfect for individuals who have a small sized balcony or as an additional Egg to another large Egg. It weighs about 80 pounds and has a diameter of 13 inches. It can cook a turkey of about 12 pounds. It is pretty portable and compatible with convEGGtor, half moon raised grid, round grill work and jalapeno grill rack.

4) **Medium:** This model is ideal for couples and new small families. Most accessories are supported by this model and it weighs about 113 pounds. It sports a diameter of 15 inches and can accommodate a turkey of 18 pounds. Best accessories for this model would be cast iron cooking grid, grid cleaner, vertical chicken roaster etc.

5) **Large:** This one the most optimal size for moderately large sized families and most gatherings. It supports most accessories as well and has a diameter of 18.25 inches with 162 pounds weight. It can hold a 20 pounds turkey and supports most accessories such as the deep dish aking stone, convEGG tore, v rack and so on.

6) **X-Large:** This particular model is best suited for large families and large friend gatherins. It allows for many meals to be cooked at same time, in fact twelve racks of ribs and 24 burgers can be made in a single session. It weights about 219 pounds and has a grid diameter of 24 inches. It has the capacity to hold 20 pound turkeys and can be used with convEGGtor, pizza peel and baking stone.

7) **XX-Large:** This is the largest one of the bunch! It is not only suitable for large family, but perfect for large parties and commercial usage, and therefore should be considered for catering groups or restaurants.

How Does The Ceramic Grill Works

The Big Green Egg actually has 4 different parts that works in conjunction to create the perfect cooking experience.

- The bottom fire box has a Flow Draft Door that follows EGG's patented design, which allows for superb air flow. The door even allows you to control the amount of air entering the appliance and fire box, giving you greater control and flexibility.
- The second part is the Fire-Box itself that uses natural lump charcoal to do its magic!
- Next, we the "Ceramic" cooking chamber that is completely air tight. This feature allows it to retain most of the heat and helps to keep the food moist and tasty.
- And finally, the multi variable "Dual" function lid made out of metal further helps to control the flow of air, while allowing you to keep the device closed for greater smoking experience.

CERAMIC GRILL TIPS

There are certain things that you should know about as they will help you to enjoy the early days of your Egg even more.

1) When using an EGG, always make sure to keep it on flat, leveled surface

2) The EGG are designed to be used with a metal nest, ensuring a gap between the egg and the bottom to allow air flow. Even if you are not using a nest, make sure to set it up in such a way that the air flow does not get obstructed.

3) Make sure to never keep your Egg on flammable surface

4) Never leave the dome opened

5) It case there are high-winds, it is highly advised that you keep a close look at your EGG while during the cooking session in order to prevent any mishaps

6) When firing up your EGG for the first time, try to prevent the EGG from reaching temperatures higher than 350 degrees F, as it will help the gasket adhesive to cure

7) Make sure to never use fluid lighter to light up your EGG. These chemicals will greatly alter the flavor of your food. Instead, try opting for BGE electric charcoal starter to light up your charcoals

8) When you are moving your Egg, first make sure that your Egg is complete cool. Never try to move a warm/hot EGG as it might cause harm to you.

9) When cooking at temperatures above 400 degrees F, try to ensure that you lift the lid about 1-2 inches prior to opening it up completely. This allows a little amount of heat to escape and prevent any self injury, this process is also known as "Burping"

DIFFERENT KINDS OF COOKING TYPES

DIRECT GRILLING

When talking about direct grilling, we are basically placing the directly over fire and cooking it by exposing it to heat and flame. It's pretty much the perfect way to cook chops, steaks, chicken breast, burgers, fillets, veggies and other simple and quick to cook foods. Basically, foods that are just tender and have a thickness of less than 2 inch are perfect for grilling directly. When you are grilling directly, you should know that it slowly sears the outer surface of your meat and forms a fine yet satisfying crust, keeping all the juices perfectly locked inside giving an amazing flavor. In fact, the meticulously designed EGG ensures that you don't get any hot spots or flare ups too! Keep in mind though, that for some food, you might need to start direct grilling at a high temperature and then lower down the heat as you go by.

INDIRECT GRILLING

When you are considering Indirect Grilling, you are essentially cooking the food using a drip pan or something similar to the convEGGtor, ensuring that the ingredient is not directly exposed to flame, but is rather cooked by heat produced at the bottom of the pan.To be more scientific, the food is cooked via convection that allows heat to radiate from the coal and dome of the EGG. This allows you to prepare rotisserie as well, as it allows the appliance rotisserie cooking as well.

SMOKING

Following the tradition, it is actually possible to Smoke meals using your EGG. Smoking using your EGG allows you to cook your meals slowly and infuse them with the smoky flavors of the wood that you are using. It allows you to slowly break down the tissues and make the meat very tender. Smoking requires a long time, for some foods smoking is done in a matter of mere minutes while for others it might take hours upon hours. The result however, would always be extremely satisfying, literally fall-off-the bone type meat with a combination of complex flavors generated by the smoke and spices that you use. Aside from the usual meat though, using the EGG you can also smoke various other types of food such as nuts, veggies, cheese and even nuts. The recommended temperature for smoking using the EGG falls somewhere around 225 degrees F to about 275 degrees F. The perfectly designed dome of the EGG makes it easier for pit masters to adjust the openings that allows for Smoke cooking.

BAKING

This is something that most people don't know about, but EGG actually allows you to use the EGG as a classical brick oven that allows you to use the EGG to make pies, biscuits, bread, pizza as so on. With absolutely precise temperature controls and heat holding capacities, it is possible to turn the EGG into the perfect baking stone! The DOME shape further helps to create a fine environment for baking while the material helps to draw the moisture and create extra-ordinary dishes!

CHAPTER-11 SMOKING MEAT

DIFFERENCE BETWEEN BARBEQUING AND SMOKING MEAT

You might not believe it, but there are still people who think that the process of Barbequing and Smoking are the same! So, this is something which you should know about before diving in deeper.

So, whenever you are going to use a traditional BBQ grill, you always put your meat directly on top of the heat source for a brief amount of time which eventually cooks up the meal. Smoking, on the other hand, will require you to combine the heat from your grill as well as the smoke to infuse a delicious smoky texture and flavor to your meat. Smoking usually takes much longer than traditional barbecuing. In most cases, it takes a minimum of 2 hours and a temperature of 100 -120 degrees for the smoke to be properly infused into the meat. Keep in mind that the time and temperature will obviously depend on the type of meat that you are using, and that is why it is suggested that you keep a meat thermometer handy to ensure that your meat is doing fine. Keep in mind that this method of barbecuing is also known as "Low and slow" smoking as well. With that cleared up, you should be aware that there are actually two different ways through which smoking is done.

THE CORE DIFFERENCE BETWEEN COLD AND HOT SMOKING

Depending on the type of grill that you are using, you might be able to get the option to go for a Hot Smoking Method or a Cold Smoking One. The primary fact about these three different cooking techniques which you should keep in mind are as follows:

- **Hot Smoking**: In this technique, the food will use both the heat on your grill and the smoke to prepare your food. This method is most suitable for items such as chicken, lamb, brisket etc.
- **Cold Smoking**: In this method, you are going to smoke your meat at a very low temperature such as 30 degree Celsius, making sure that it doesn't come into the direct contact with the heat. This is mostly used as a means to preserve meat and extend their life on the shelf.
- **Roasting Smoke**: This is also known as Smoke Baking. This process is essentially a combined form of both roasting and baking and can be performed in any type of smoker with a capacity of reaching temperatures above 82 degree Celsius.

By now you must be really curious to know about the different types of Smokers that are out there right?

Well, in the next section I am exactly going to discuss that!

THE DIFFERENT TYPES OF AVAILABLE SMOKERS

Essentially, what you should know is that right now in the market, you are going to get three different types of Smokers.

Charcoal Smoker

These types of smokers are hands down the best one for infusing the perfect Smoky flavor to your meat. But be warned, though, that these smokers are a little bit difficult to master as the method of regulating temperature is a little bit difficult when compared to normal Gas or Electric smokers.

Electric Smoker

After the charcoal smoker, next comes perhaps the simpler option, Electric Smokers. These are easy to use and plug and play type. All you need to do is just plug in, set the temperature and go about your daily life. The smoker will do the rest. However, keep in mind that the finishing smoky flavor won't be as intense as the Charcoal one.

Gas Smokers

Finally, comes the Gas Smokers. These have a fairly easy mechanism for temperature control and are powered usually by LP Gas. The drawback of these Smokers is that you are going to have to keep checking up on your Smoker every now and then to ensure that it has not run out of Gas.

Now, these have been further dissected into different styles of the smoker. Each of which is preferred by Smokers of different experiences.

THE DIFFERENT STYLES OF SMOKERS

The different styles of Smokers are essentially divided into the following.

Vertical (Bullet Style Using Charcoal)
These are usually low-cost solutions and are perfect for first-time smokers.

Vertical (Cabinet Style)
These Smokers come with a square shaped design with cabinets and drawers/trays for easy accessibility. These cookers also come with a water tray and a designated wood chips box as well.

Offset
These type of smokers have dedicated fireboxes that are attached to the side of the main grill. The smoke and heat required for these are generated from the firebox itself which is then passed through the main chamber and out through a nicely placed chimney.

Kamado Joe
And finally, we have the Kamado Joe which is ceramic smokers are largely regarded as being the "Jack Of All Trades".

These smokers can be used as low and slow smokers, grills, hi or low-temperature ovens and so on.

They have a very thick ceramic wall which allows it to hold heat better than any other type of smoker out there, requiring only a little amount of charcoal. These are easy to use with better insulation and are more efficient when it comes to fuel control.

With the smokers now set up, the next step is to understand about the woods used in the smoker. Below is a table which discusses most of the general types of woods that are used in Smokers and their potential benefits.

THE DIFFERENT TYPES OF WOOD AND THEIR BENEFITS

The Different Types Of Wood	Suitable For
Hickory	Wild game, chicken, pork, cheeses, beef
Pecan	Chicken, pork, lamb, cheeses, fish.
Mesquite	Beef and vegetables
Alder	Swordfish, Salmon, Sturgeon and other types of fishes. Works well with pork and chicken too.
Oak	Beef or briskets
Maple	Vegetable, ham or poultry
Cherry	Game birds, poultry or pork
Apple	Game birds, poultry, beef
Peach	Game birds, poultry or pork
Grape Vines	Beef, chicken or turkey
Wine Barrel Chips	Turkey, beef, chicken or cheeses
Seaweed	Lobster, mussels, crab, shrimp etc.
Herbs or Spices such as rosemary, bay leaves, mint, lemon peels, whole nutmeg etc.	Good for cheeses or vegetables and a small collection of light meats such as fillets or fish steaks.

THE BASIC PREPARATIONS

- Always be prepared to spend the whole day and take as much time as possible to smoke your meat for maximum effect.
- Make sure to obtain the perfect Ribs/Meat for the meal which you are trying to smoke. Do a little bit of research if you need.
- I have already added a list of woods in this book, consult to that list and choose the perfect wood for your meal.
- Make sure to prepare the marinade for each of the meals properly. A great deal of the flavor comes from the rubbing.
- Keep a meat thermometer handy to get the internal temperature when needed.
- Use mittens or tongs to keep yourself safe
- Refrain yourself from using charcoal infused alongside starter fluid as it might bring a very unpleasant odor to your food
- Always make sure to start off with a small amount of wood and keep adding them as you cook.
- Don't be afraid to experiment with different types of wood for newer flavor and experiences.
- Always keep a notebook near you and note jot down whatever you are doing or learning and use them during the future session. This will help you to evolve and move forward.

THE CORE ELEMENTS OF SMOKING!

Smoking is a very indirect method of cooking that relies on a number of different factors to give you the most perfectly cooked meal that you are looking for. Each of these components is very important to the whole process as they all work together to create the meal of your dreams.

- **Time**: Unlike grilling or even Barbequing, smoking takes a really long time and requires a whole lot of patience. It takes time for the smoky flavor to slowly get infused into the meats. Jus to bring things into comparison, it takes an about 8 minutes to fully cook a steak through direct heating, while smoking (indirect heating) will take around 35-40 minutes.

- **Temperature:** When it comes to smoking, the temperature is affected by a lot of different factors that are not only limited to the wind, cold air temperatures but also the cooking wood's dryness. Some smokers work best with large fires that are controlled by the draw of a chimney and restricted airflow through the various vents of the cooking chamber and firebox. While other smokers tend to require smaller fire with fewer coals as well as a completely different combination of the vent and draw controls. However, most smokers are designed to work at temperatures as low as 180 degrees Fahrenheit to as high as 300 degrees Fahrenheit. But the recommend temperature usually falls between 250 degrees Fahrenheit and 275 degrees Fahrenheit.

- **Airflow:** The level of air to which the fire is exposed to greatly determines how your fire will burn and how quickly it will burn the fuel. For instance, if you restrict air flow into the firebox by closing up the available vents, then the fire will burn at a low temperature and vice versa. Typically in smokers, after lighting up the fire, the vents are opened to allow for maximum air flow and is then adjusted throughout the cooking process to make sure that optimum flame is achieved.

- **Insulation:** Insulation is also very important when it comes to smokers as it helps to easily manage the cooking process throughout the whole cooking session. A good insulation allows smokers to efficiently reach the desired temperature instead of waiting for hours upon hours!

CONCLUSION

I can't express how honored I am to think that you found my book interesting and informative enough to read it all through to the end. I thank you again for purchasing this book and I hope that you had as much fun reading it as I had writing it. I bid you farewell and encourage you to move forward and find your true Smoked Meat spirit!

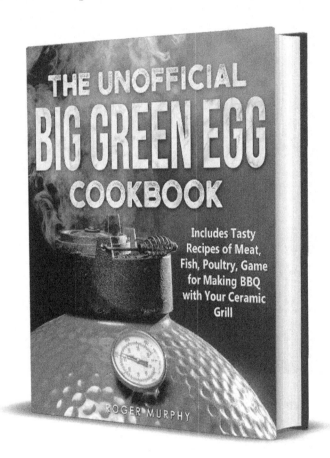

GET YOUR FREE GIFT

Subscribe to our Mail List and get your FREE copy of the book

'Smoking Meat: The Best 20 Recipes of Smoked Meat, Unique Recipes for Unique BBQ'

https://tiny.cc/smoke20

OTHER BOOKS BY ADAM JONES

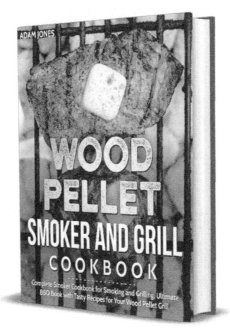

https://www.amazon.com/gp/product/1070936340

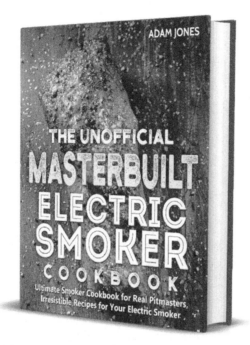

https://www.amazon.com/dp/1098708040

P.S. Thank you for reading this book. If you've enjoyed this book, please don't shy, drop me a line, leave a review or both on Amazon. I love reading reviews and your opinion is extremely important for me.

My Amazon page: www.amazon.com/author/adjones

Made in the USA
Coppell, TX
06 June 2021